SHARING
YOUR
FAITH
WITH A
HINDU

This book may be kept
Twenty-one days
A fine of $0.20 per day will
be charged for each day it is overdue

SHARING
YOUR
FAITH
WITH A
HINDU

MADASAMY
THIRUMALAI

BETHANYHOUSE
MINNEAPOLIS, MINNESOTA

Published by Bethany House Publishers
A Ministry of Bethany Fellowship International
11400 Hampshire Avenue South
Bloomington, Minnesota 55438
www.bethanyhouse.com

Printed in the United States of America by
Bethany Press International, Bloomington, Minnesota 55438

Library of Congress Cataloging-in-Publication Data

Thirumalai, M. S., 1940-
    Sharing your faith with a Hindu / by Madasamy Thirumalai.
      p. cm.
Includes bibliographical references (p.).
    ISBN 0-7642-2632-0
    1. Missions to Hindus. I. Title.
    BV3265.3 .T47   2002
    266'.0088'2945—dc21   2002002472

MADASAMY THIRUMALAI is a professor of world religions and linguistics, and the academic dean at Bethany College of Missions, has taught at universities in India, and is a widely published author. A native of India, he has a master's degree from the University of Hawaii, and a Ph.D. in linguistics from the University of Calcutta. He and his family live near Minneapolis, Minnesota.

CONTENTS

PREFACE

I have personally experienced the grace of the Lord Jesus Christ through my friends while writing this book. Mike Leeming, Professor of Missions and Biblical Studies at Bethany College of Missions, read the entire manuscript and made several suggestions to improve its presentation. My wife, Swarna, read portions of the manuscript in several stages and helped improve its quality and the information and analysis presented here. My friends Stan and Vangie Schmidt, Steve and Denise Darula, Hoinu and Dave Bunce, and John and Michelle Pandian, who have abiding interest in India and who alway pray for the salvation of Hindus, were a great source of strength and encouragement.

I have benefited greatly from the interesting conversations I had with my many colleagues Ed Dudek, Paul Hartford, Tom Shetler, Dennis Stein, and Nita Steiner on the methods of evangelism discussed in this book. I am very glad to make special mention of Alec Brooks, Paul Strand, Joel Anantharaz, and Seelan Mathiaparanam, who took special interest in this project and helped me with insights based upon their field experience.

It is an honor to publish through Bethany House Publishers, a ministry wholly dedicated to the spread of the gospel of Jesus Christ all over the world. I owe gratitude and appreciation to Gary and Carol Johnson, the devoted leaders of this organization, and to Steve Laube, Julie Smith, Christopher Soderstrom, and Karen Madison for all their help.

My prayer is that this book will help its readers to gaze at the beauty and grace of our Lord and Savior, Jesus Christ, and enable them to take a step forward in sharing their faith with their Hindu neighbors.

—M. S. Thirumalai

INTRODUCTION

I was brought up a Hindu in a small town in southern India. I believed in and worshiped idols, and I sought the favors of gods and spirits through animal sacrifices, sorcery, divination, and witchcraft.

My parents came from a middle caste of agriculturists; they devoted their time and money to Hindu gods and goddesses. They would also occasionally visit the Darga (Muslim shrines) to obtain physical or mental healing, and they always showed great respect and deference to the Brahman priests in our own temples.

Some people from my caste living in other villages and towns had embraced Christianity. Now, we believed that every religion had some truth to offer so embracing another religion wasn't a problem. However, it was shameful and degrading to become a *Christian*, especially because so many people from lower castes had placed their faith in Jesus Christ. We thought they had become Christians through some type of compulsion or inducement.

As a child, I felt that the Christians with whom I came into contact were more interested in each other than in us. Even so, when I was in the fifth grade, as I was helping my father in his vegetable store, a simple-looking lady offered me a storybook in my own language. I accepted it with my father's permission; it happened to be Luke's gospel.

I read it with great enthusiasm, and I instantaneously admired the authority, majesty, and compassion of the man Jesus. It took many years for me to come to seek the Lord Jesus Christ with all my heart, and then to speak boldly of His love for us all. As an educated person, it also took time for me to shed my feeling of shame in being a Christian.

The name of Jesus is alive. Thousands like me are hearing of Him, and many are beginning to admit that He is gracious, caring, mighty, and worthy of worship. The Holy Spirit stirs desire in the hearts of the people He has created, and these stirrings in the hearts of Hindus need to be nourished. It is my hope and prayer that this book will serve the function of helping us to become co-laborers with the Spirit in His ministry of saving souls.

India's population passed the one billion mark in 2001, and in about five to eight years it will surpass China as the world's most populous nation. The Indian Census Office states that 82 percent of the people in India are Hindus; in other words, there are already more than 820 million Hindus in India. Add to this the millions of native Hindus in Nepal (the only country that declares itself to be a Hindu nation), Pakistan, Bangladesh, Sri Lanka, and some Indonesian islands, as well as the overseas Indian populations—the Hindu Diaspora (dispersion or scattering of people)—in Malaysia, Singapore, the West Indies, South Africa, other African nations, Britain, the Fiji Islands, Mauritius, the Reunion Islands, and recent immigrants to Europe, Australia, Canada, and the United States.

The influence Hindus have over people of other faiths and traditions, especially secularized Christians, rationalists, academics, politicians, and professionals, continues to grow. Hinduism is the third-largest religion in the world, with about 900 million people professing their loyalty. (Christianity is the largest, with 1.973 billion followers, and Islam is second, with 1.27 billion.)

INCREASE OF HINDU PRESENCE IN THE UNITED STATES

The last three decades have seen tremendous growth in the presence of Hindus in the United States. Most metropolitan cities have Hindu temples, and Hindu centers are found everywhere. Yoga has come into the mainstream of medical practice and into the day-to-day regimen of meditation and exercise. It is estimated that 1.4 million people of Indian origin live in the United States; of these, more than 85 percent (1.2 million) are Hindus.

In the United States, Hindus are earning a reputation as a skilled community, seeking higher education and employment in high-tech sectors; a recent news report appearing in major papers around the country said that of the estimated 1.4 million Indians now in the United States, some 400,000—nearly a third!—hold such positions. The report also said that skilled Indian professionals are immigrating into the United States at a rate of more than fifty thousand a year.

MISSION WORK IN INDIA

While India in general, and the Hindu religion in particular, have remained mysterious to the Christian church for centuries, no other religion or nation has received so much focused attention or resources from missionaries via the church than the Hindu religion and the Indian subcontinent. Indian Christians believe that the apostle Thomas preached the gospel in India and was martyred there. The Indian Church does have an unbroken recorded history of at least one thousand years, and India has witnessed some spectacular mass movements to Christ; however, at the end of the twentieth century, the Indian government estimated the number of Christians in India at only about thirty million, or 3 percent.

SLOW CHURCH GROWTH

Missionaries and other evangelists have always noted the laborious growth of the church in India, in spite of favorable conditions for conversion in the past. This observation provoked the Jesuit missionary Abbé Dubois, who labored for Christ for nearly thirty years and brought thousands into the Catholic fold in southern India, to declare in 1815 that the time for the Hindus to accept Jesus Christ as Lord and Savior had already passed, and that they would rather turn to secular atheism than to God.

In the second half of the twentieth century, it looked as if even ever-optimistic, prayerful Christians had lost their hope for a change of heart among the Hindus. At the end of World War II, the Western church began turning its attention more toward the countries of the Iron Curtain, and more recently toward Islamic nations. In other words, the geopolitical attention of the body of Christ shifted from the former British colonies to the countries under direct communist rule and Islamic fundamentalism. Meanwhile, *Hindu* missionaries took advantage of the estrangement between younger generations and the Christian church and firmly established themselves by offering alternative approaches to spirituality. Because there were no great efforts at checkmating the spread of animism and pantheism, Hinduism became an influential force in Western thinking and ways of life.

AN ENIGMA

The Hindu faith continues to remain puzzling; it includes theological positions that are contradictory to one another and yet coexist under the same umbrella. Hinduism is an unusual religion in that it caters to every taste and persuasion; it is also unusual in that millions of Hindus do not really know for certain what Hinduism is all about. Even in their confusion, Hindus devotedly and almost unfailingly follow rituals and disciplines handed down to them through oral traditions for thousands of years. There is no explicit creed or dogma that unifies the various segments, sects, and denominations that claim to be part of the Hindu religion; even atheism is a recognized and respectable element! Ultimately, in the strictest sense, Hinduism is more a way of life than a religion, and the kaleidoscopic experience offered by the Hindu faith becomes the chief deadly attraction to the modern Western mind, nurtured in a civilization of individual adventurism.

Hinduism is even willing to accept the divinity of Jesus as a possibility, while at the same time vehemently resisting and rejecting His sovereignty and exclusive saving grace. It presents the attractive proposition that man can become God and glorifies the individual, encouraging him to seek his salvation on his own terms; it declares that the individual can achieve anything if she sets her mind upon achieving her goal. Modern Hinduism accepts the language of contemporary psychology and uses it as part of its theological exposition at the intellectual level.

Hinduism is the most accommodating of all religions. In a world full of strife, the "accommodative" spirit and the planks of universalism and relativism, as well as the other cultivated characteristics of modern Hinduism, become very attractive to so many diverse groups of people that the Hindus have truly come to see their faith as a relevant global religion. This sense of importance, as well as pride in the ancestral past, continues to help encourage the intellectual Hindu to hold on to his religion and resist the invitation of Christ.

TYPES OF HINDUS

The Hindu who is devoted to daily rituals thinks that they are sufficient to ensure his salvation. Often he occupies a preeminent position within the social hierarchy. His manifest demonstration and performance of daily rituals in public areas and places of worship fortifies this status. He is very much devoted to the idols he worships and serves; he may at times acknowledge that the god he worships may not reside in the idol, but often he behaves as if his god and his idol are one and the same. Service to the idol becomes service to his god.

Intellectual Hinduism provides the rationale for Hindu beliefs and practices. Heavily dependent on nationalism, patriotism, and traditions, intellectually oriented Hindus develop their worldview and the scheme of salvation through karma, reincarnation, and performance of caste duties (defined later).

Folk Hinduism is representative of the millions of Hindus who do not even know the existence or names of their ancient scriptural texts; these put their entire trust for religious and spiritual pursuits in the leadership of the priestly class. They also build their own community/caste temples and offer all kinds of sacrifices; they believe in the rituals, and they seek priests to perform them for their benefit. While they stand or kneel or prostrate themselves in reverence and awe before the idols, and while they may even make supplications to the gods in their own language, they still need the services of the priests to perform the ritual worship through recitations in the ancient Sanskrit language, which they do not speak or understand. While the priestly class is believed to be a social group superior to the rest, the millions of folk Hindus often quarrel among themselves as to their relative social rank.

There are scores of ethnic communities or "tribes," some numbering a million or more people, whose belief systems may closely resemble that of the folk Hindus. However, these tribes do not fall within the caste structure of Hindu communities and have been kept traditionally outside the perimeter of the Hindu religion. Many among these have come to know Jesus as Lord and Savior, although a large section have not yet been reached with the gospel. In recent times there have been attempts made by Hindu activists to bring Christians among these ethnic groups back to Hinduism.

Finally, there is a growing number of secular Hindus who continue to accept the identity of Hinduism but who emphasize the importance of the humanistic basis of the religion. These people may be primarily concerned with the social and economic development of the Hindu masses, or simply interested in their own and their family's economic progress. Impacted by science and rationalism, they may recognize the importance of Hinduism's spiritual elements but not the rituals.

The sects of Hinduism are many and varied, but when it comes to evangelizing them, most seem to respond in a similar manner—they resist the gospel. However, one should not fail to notice the differences in receptivity to the Good News based on regional and caste factors. It is possible that such variance in openness to the truth among the different areas and social groups may be accentuated by the depth and intensity of gospel work among them.

THE PURPOSE OF SHARING YOUR FAITH WITH A HINDU

My intent in writing this book is to help Christians in the United States and Europe to share their faith with Hindus who live in their neighborhoods, as well as those with whom they come in contact in everyday social settings or workplaces.

To present the gospel of Jesus Christ to someone only requires a willingness to obey and follow the call of the Holy Spirit. If we allow ourselves to be a willing tool, He will show us how to converse with our Hindu neighbors and help them come to know Jesus as their Lord and Savior. In the process, we must learn some of the major theological constructs of Hinduism in order to answer the genuine concerns and interests of our Hindu friends. Notions of karma, samsara, the Hindu stages of life, ideas or ways of salvation, attitudes toward other religions and faiths, trends in modern Hinduism, yoga, Transcendental Meditation (TM) and other disciplines, objections to the exclusive claim of the divinity of Christ, and socio-cultural concerns of accepting Jesus will all be raised by them. We should respond to these questions sincerely and in simple terms that they can relate to and understand.

Conversion of the heart is never brought about by facts and arguments. True conversion is accomplished by the ministry of the Holy

Spirit and not by any human being or human books, including this one. Firmly believing in the work of the Spirit, we will benefit by a non-technical presentation of the concepts of the Christian faith.

This book focuses on the personal steps that an average Western Christian can take to help her Hindu neighbor to come to know the saving grace of Jesus Christ, and through this process, also reach the Hindus of India. These steps will be different for different groups of Hindus, although the basic preparation on our part, namely, fasting and prayer, as well as trust in and dependence on the continuing work of the Holy Spirit, are the same for all groups.

The following chapters present (1) the general profiles of Hindus, (2) the concerns that a Hindu may have when we approach him or her with the gospel, (3) possible answers to these concerns, and (4) tips and methods for reaching out to Hindus as well as general conduct toward Hindus. Reading these chapters will give Christians insight into the specific religious spectrum to which their particular Hindu friends belong; this helps believers not to generalize but to focus on the specific needs and profiles of their Hindu acquaintances. This book will help the average Christian not only to visit Hindus in their homes but also to receive them and extend hospitality in an appropriate manner. In general, the chapters are written with an eye on appropriate social response as well as tips for presenting the gospel.

The social ills of Hinduism have been highlighted in many other publications, and these often come to the surface while discussing Hinduism, both among Christians and with Hindus. Such focused descriptions may further antagonize Hindus we meet in Western nations. The eradication of social injustice, for example, is a legitimate concern for any well-meaning Christian, but it should not be allowed as a stumbling block to sharing the gospel with Hindus.

My primary focus is on nudging Hindus toward understanding and accepting the role of Jesus in their lives. It is important for us to understand, at least partially, what they believe before we approach them with the Good News. I believe in the dynamic role of the Holy Spirit, who teaches all of us to look at one another as people created in the image of God.

WHO IS A HINDU?

1

Who *is a Hindu?* and *What is Hinduism?* are questions that defy any precise answer for scholars and laypeople alike. Christians in the West find it difficult to understand Hinduism because they do not see any central or essential creed that permeates the entire faith, and they do not see a founder or founders of Hinduism. There is no single universally accepted religious text, and there is no uniform code of conduct.

There are also no universally followed perceptual markers that distinguish a Hindu from a non-Hindu. An observant Jew has a skullcap, and an observant Muslim sports a beard, but many Hindu men who work in public places no longer have the traditional markers on their foreheads or bodies. Hindu women do continue to wear auspicious dots on their foreheads, and Roman Catholic women also follow this practice in India.

Christians in the West often take all Hindus to be vegetarians and practitioners of yoga, but the vast majority of Hindus are non-vegetarians, and most never practice yoga. Westerners also think that Hindus do not eat beef because of the "sacred cow," but millions of Hindus from the so-called lower social strata are beefeaters. Westerners may tend to dismiss Hinduism as nothing but animism, a form of primitive religion propelled by the fear of natural phenomena. But some of the best expressions of human thought and philosophy are embraced and represented in Hinduism. For example, Saivism (the sect that worships Shiva as the primary god) and Vaishnavism (the sect that worships Vishnu as the primary god) place great stress on the grace of the Supreme Being. Intellectual Hinduism is known for its philosophical search for God and His grace.

THE HINDU VIEW OF HINDUISM

It's not only the outsider who finds it difficult to define a Hindu; the Hindus themselves acknowledge that they are so different from one another that it is almost impossible for them to define who they are. However, they also know that there is no need to define themselves for the benefit of others because they claim that *they* know what they are. They marvel at the variety of religious practices and beliefs that their "religion" or their "way" tolerates, encourages, and accepts. They are amazed at the variety of gods they worship, at the audacity of their materialist philosophers and their followers who deny the existence of gods and yet are part of their religion, the variety of languages they use, and the cultures, marital customs, and food habits they practice. They admire the tenacity of their religion to survive, and they feel proud that despite being ruled by people of other religions for a thousand years, their faith continues. They know that their "strength" lies in toleration of all faiths, in accepting the beliefs and gods that suit their genius, temper, and convenience, by providing a berth for all under the Hindu sun. They acknowledge that their social stratification is perhaps outmoded but insist that it has existed with the "willing" participation of all, including the most oppressed, and has been slowly changing. They know that there may be some truth in every idea they encounter: Take what suits you best and leave the rest as it is.

SOME CHARACTERISTICS OF HINDUS

Let us identify some of the essential common characteristics of Hindus. Remember that any attempt to fully characterize Hindus will always be an oversimplification.

(1) *Hindus are primarily from India.* Even so, as mentioned, Nepal is the only country that declares Hinduism to be its official religion. Also, there are Hindus of native stock in the Indonesian islands—these adopted Hinduism over a thousand years ago through the political and religious activities of Hindus from India. The Hindu religion lives through the Buddhist faith and rituals in almost every

Southeast Asian country, and there are many Hindus in various areas around the world (see chapter 1).

The Hindu population in Pakistan has been dwindling in recent years, though Hindu immigration to the affluent West is growing every year. The Hindus from British India who migrated to other lands were often small-time traders, service providers, or indentured laborers, and were less educated and poor. However, as previously stated, the recent immigrants are mostly from the educated classes with a penchant for business, medical, engineering, and other lucrative careers. While most of these people are still in the role of providing services rather than being independent entrepreneurs, the newest generation has taken to information technology like fish to water.

While the immigrants from British India took with them the folk religious beliefs and practices and only a vague idea of intellectual Hinduism, recent immigrants are relatively better informed about classical text based Hinduism. They are also a product of a free and intensely independent nation, socio-politically fluent and articulate, and ready for debate. Conversion to Hinduism is not widespread, but we do hear of some people converting from primal religions in various parts of India as well as from secular groups. We also sometimes hear of re-conversions from Islam and Christianity to Hinduism, publicized widely by Hindu political groups. When such deliberate conversions are introduced, people adopt a mixture of folk beliefs and rituals of classical Hindu religion. Converts from the West usually are initiated into text-based Hindu religion, with a dose of the everyday rituals generally practiced by upper-caste Hindus.

(2) *Hindus worship idols, images, pictures, relics, and other objects.* There may be groups of people among Hindus who refrain from worshiping idols, but none could be considered iconoclastic (completely against idols). Even if they do not worship such objects, their reverence for the idols, images, pictures, relics, and other objects is very strong and often distinguishes Hindus clearly from other religious groups. Hindu temples follow a daily routine of rituals that may include waking up, bathing, feeding, garlanding, and putting to bed the idols or images. There are other rituals that reflect the eras of life of the gods, such as marriage ceremonies between gods and goddesses, birthday celebrations, and sacrifices. There are also ceremonies that are performed according to the seasons of the Hindu calendar and other astronomical calculations; for example, certain new-moon

days are considered to be very important. Hindu respect for elders, living saints (gurus), dead relatives, and leaders can easily evolve into worship.

(3) *Hindus believe in rebirth and karma.* All living organisms—humans, animals, and plants—are said to constitute a binding soul-kinship. A human being who dies today will be reborn until he reaches the stage of total liberation from the continuing cycle of birth, death, and rebirth; he may return as a human being, an animal, or a plant in his next birth—his form and status depend upon his acts of commission and omission in the life he just completed and upon the merit he accumulated through good and evil deeds in the present life as well as the lives he led previously.

Belief in rebirth and karma (defined simply as the thoughts, words, and deeds that have a consequence for one's placement in the next life) is not a mere theological point; it has extremely serious social consequences for the Hindu individual and for society. Since one's thoughts, words, and deeds in this life have consequences in the next life, what you are now is the result of what you were before. The Hindu social hierarchy and divisions receive their sustenance mainly from this set of beliefs.

(4) *Hindus are pantheistic, polytheistic (actually henotheistic), and animistic practitioners of religion.* Hindus may see their Supreme Being in every object; the entire creation, including humans, animals, and plants, is all part of the Supreme Being. Generally speaking, salvation for a Hindu is seeking union with this Supreme Being, liberated from the clutches of the cycles of birth, death, and rebirth; he generally sees his body to be a burden in this pursuit.

In some ways, a Hindu believes that everything is god (*pantheism*). While an intellectual Hindu does recognize the immanence as well as the transcendence of god, the majority of Hindus are governed by efforts seeking god's immanence. The Supreme Being is identified with nature, the creation; the distinction between creator and creation is rather blurred in Hinduism, as finite objects are identified with the infinite God. Hindus worship gods of different creeds, cults, or peoples, and in this way, they tolerate the worship of all gods: The universe as a whole becomes god.

Hindus are also *polytheistic*, believing in pantheons of gods. Most Christians notice that Hindus present a contradictory picture of seeming to believe in both monotheism (one God) and polytheism (many gods) at the same time. Hindus do recognize the existence of one Supreme Being, but they also believe that this one Supreme Being may appear to humans in different forms, and an individual Hindu may choose to worship one god or another—this, specifically, is henotheism, a sub-view of polytheism.

Hindus believe that there are countless gods; traditional sayings or estimates put the number in the millions. These gods are formed or viewed as representing natural forces and objects such as fertility, rain, and fire; vegetation such as trees and plants; animals such as cows, serpents, and eagles; animal/human combinations; and abstract qualities such as love, education, disease, healing, and agriculture.

However, there are also Hindu sects and individuals that focus on the worship of only one god, while acknowledging the existence and possibility of worshiping more than one god simultaneously. Gods are visualized to constitute a society of their own, which parallels human society in several ways: Gods get married and beget children, for instance; many of them have their own personal vehicles, mostly animals and birds, for transportation.

Again, an interesting aspect of Hindu polytheism is that an individual may believe in one god as the deity of the tribe, community, or individual without asserting that this god is the only god. He believes that one supreme god reveals himself through several local or lesser gods. Worshiping such local or lesser gods with devotion may be just as meritorious as worshiping the Supreme Being (again, this is called henotheism).

Hindus are likewise *animistic*, believing in, depending on, and worshiping spirit beings, sacred animals, birds, and humans; they also worship the spirits of dead relatives through offerings. While the ancestor-worship practices of the Hindus are not as elaborate as those of the Chinese, annual remembrance is common. Charms, talismans, and fetishes are used; Hindus flock to the shamans, fortune-tellers, astrologers, gurus, and priests to receive information about their future, to ameliorate their suffering, and to take remedial action against the evil designs of the Enemy, known or unknown. Hindus fear the dead and conciliate them for the welfare of the living.

Magic and divination are an integral part of folk Hindu practices, and ordeal is an accepted form of worship of the family deity. Telepathy, witchcraft, and sorcery are all employed; note, however, that not all Hindus indulge in these practices. There is a strong sense of cynicism among modern educated Hindus about these things, while at the same time seeking the counsel and insight of the guru is one of their favorite pastimes.

(5) *Hindus are usually governed by the social system of caste.* The Code of Manu, written perhaps in the fifth century B.C., classifies Hindu society as consisting of four social divisions in the following descending order of rank: Brahman, the priestly class; Kshatriya, the military class; Vaisya, the agriculturist and business class; and Sudra, the servant class. A fifth class of people was created over the centuries, consisting of the so-called untouchables, the lowest position in Hindu society. These five classes or categories are further subdivided into specific castes, numbered into the thousands. While every caste may accord the highest rank to the Brahmans, ranking among the other castes often is a bone of contention among them.

The net result of the caste system is that man's station in life is fixed from birth according to the caste into which he is born. If an individual is born into the carpenter caste, for example, he is expected to pursue the profession of a carpenter; if he is born into the barber's caste, he is expected to pursue the profession of a barber. If he does not follow the avocation assigned to his caste, he is transgressing and committing a sin for which he will face serious consequences in his future rebirth. Modern educational systems fortunately allow people the chance to overcome this barrier, and yet the Hindus belonging to lower castes often feel that they are discriminated against. In the past, educational opportunities to the lower castes either were not provided or were ignored. The karmic injunction that one should only pursue the work that is ordained by the caste system is no longer taken as seriously as it once was. However, the consequences of this belief system are felt in the present day—many among the lower castes do not have any desire to send their children to school because their ethos never saw this as a fitting caste duty for them.

An individual's worldview is colored by his caste upbringing; he sees the suffering and successes of his own caste more readily, he seeks support and succor from his caste leadership for jobs and investments, and he may vote for his own caste candidate just because he belongs to it.

The caste system does not encourage inter-caste marriage. However, while Hinduism may not encourage inter-caste dining, modern laws now make it a cognizable offense if people from the so-called untouchable castes are ill treated in public places and institutions. It should be mentioned that intense and publicly exhibited caste feeling is actually found more among the non-Brahman castes than among the Brahmans. Caste, despite its acknowledged evil influence, has come to stay among the Hindus. In the Code of Manu, it is actually said that for sins of thought in his previous birth and in his previous body, a man is born into the lowest caste. Karma extends crucial support to the caste institution in terms of commonly accepted Hindu theology.

(6) *Hindus are known for their tolerance and acceptance of a wide variety of theological beliefs from within their religion.* As an extreme example, atheism is viewed as a religious-philosophical belief and pursuit of atheism is acceptable within Hinduism. Likewise, denying the power and importance of gods not of one's own sect is quite common. Sometimes it is also held that the very same god or Supreme Being is found in every sect in different forms. But one may negate the existence of god or Supreme Being and still be considered a Hindu.

Hindu tolerance and acceptance of a variety of theological beliefs emanating from within their religion may also extend to their tolerance of other religions and faiths. For example, there is a widespread belief that all religions lead to the same Supreme Being, just as all rivers reach and are merged into the ocean. Hindus recognize the existence of other religions and are rather willing to allow these religions to exist and continue; this does not mean, however, that they see and acknowledge them as a valid path.

Hindu recognition of other religions has not led to widespread conversions among Hindus. In reality, acceptance of the position that all religions lead to God has helped keep Hindus together in the Hindu fold and helped resist conversions to other religions. Hinduism may receive influence from other religions, but it is nonetheless a closed system. The Hindu religion is a conglomerate of a number of belief systems; the variety of views comes from the fact that the religion is pantheistic as well as polytheistic.

(7) *Continuity, not change, dominates the concerns of Hindus.* Hindus consider their religion to be an eternal religion, *sanatana dharma*, with no beginning, no end, and no founder. Hinduism, though, has undergone tremendous changes in its theology through the centuries. With the introduction of imperial Islam a thousand

years ago, a concerted Christian missionary penetration, and the political rule of the British for a few hundred years, the Hindus have been exposed to opposite views and have had their due share of reform movements. Even so, throughout these currents of history, Hinduism sees for itself a continuity of thought while renewing itself from within through the impact of these influences.

The average Hindu seeks continuity and security in his life; he is governed by what he has learned from his parents and grandparents and the community of which he is part. Changing a convention or practice is hard for him, although changes do take place. A Hindu usually has a very strong sense of respect for the institutions to which he belongs; the caste system has provided continuity and security. With the advent of modern schooling, barriers *are* being broken between the castes in public places, and a spirit of enterprise is taking hold of Hindus. But in spite of changes in economic-social relations, there is a strong tendency to preserve the "best" in the Hindu tradition. The highly educated Hindu sees the need to go back to his traditions even while he takes advantage of modern systems of education.

(8) *As in other religions, there is a vast gulf between the elitist and folk religious forms and practices of Hinduism.* However, Hindus view folk religion with greater sympathy, and its practices dominate the religious life of the vast majority. For the Westerner, there may not be any discernible difference between the folk and elitist religious practices of the Hindu—both forms focus on idol worship; however, Hindus instinctively distinguish between the two. The scriptural or elitist religion is highly respected, but for convenience, it is the folk religion that is usually followed.

Hinduism has been organized so that in the past the study of the Hindu sacred texts was not open to the lower classes. With no access to the scriptures, and with pantheistic and polytheistic approaches to the Supreme Being, the average Hindu is more easily governed by the folk traditions. He is very devoted to the family deity and family temple. Family and caste traditions become intertwined with religious beliefs and practices.

When Hindus migrated as indentured labor in the nineteenth century, they often carried with them the only caste or family religion they knew. As a result, even now they worship the gods and celebrate the festivals and holy days more akin to the folk religious practices. At the same time, every group acknowledges the superiority of the elitist, scripture-based religion. When people of different castes and communities come together, it is the text-based religion that is often followed.

RITUAL HINDUS

2

Aritual Hindu usually comes from the priestly caste called Brahman or Brahmin, and it is universally acknowledged by Hindus that the Brahmans are the highest ranked of all Hindu castes. However, since Hinduism traditionally has prescribed various rituals to be followed by different castes, a ritual Hindu may also be found among the other castes.

A Brahman is required to perform prescribed rituals at regular intervals during the day. He starts the day with a bath in a river or a fountain or any water source (now even in the bathroom of his house), and along with his bath he recites Sanskrit verses from the ancient Vedas, verses that are appropriate for the morning session. He is acquainted with these writings early in his life, and he undergoes ceremonious initiation to the priestly community through prescribed rituals. He is calm and quiet and usually mechanical about the recitation of verses, making offerings to various high gods of Hinduism. He also guards himself against pollution by not eating food offered by those not belonging to his caste.

It is possible that he may opt to become a priest himself, but often those families among the ritual Hindus who are traditionally connected to the temples perform the priestly duties. Often the ritual Hindu understands the meaning of the verses he recites, but of course many recite the verses without understanding their meaning or importance. He is conscious that he is from a high caste, but he may or may not take advantage of this position. Regardless, he is zealous about the purity and higher rank of his caste; he is the true backbone of Hinduism, and he feels guilty if he does not perform the rituals.

Others may malign him, but he is aware of his role as the preserver of the Hindu way of life.

Some Important Rituals

The rituals followed are manifold: these may be daily routine rituals, rituals connected with the seasons of life (the human life cycle), or socially required rituals. Rituals are usually performed both in the morning and in the evening.

Childhood rituals are numerous: the naming ceremony on the tenth or the twelfth day after birth, the ceremony to begin eating solid food, an ear-piercing ceremony, and the first haircutting ceremony are some examples.

The ritual of initiation (*upanayana*) is performed in adolescence, usually done at the age of eight for the Brahmans, at eleven for those belonging to soldiers' (Kshatriya) castes, and at twelve for those belonging to the business (Vaisya) castes. This is perhaps the most important ritual in the life of an upper-caste Hindu because the individual's place in the caste hierarchy is established at this time; initiation is considered to be the second birth. Initiation of persons belonging to the fourth category of castes (Sudra) or the fifth category of casteless groups ("untouchables") is not allowed—they have only one physical birth in the present life.

The teacher who conducts the initiation ceremony imparts the sacred text Veda to the one who is being initiated, the one who is supposed to be born again in the Veda. The boy being initiated is given a sacred thread consisting of three cords (for the Brahmans) that is worn over the left shoulder and hangs under the right arm. This sacred thread becomes an extremely important sign in the life of the individual because it always reminds him of his caste identity, his religious duty, and his place in the social hierarchy among the Hindus. Only rarely do we see Brahman boys not wearing the sacred thread.

The initiation ceremony is celebrated with great enthusiasm, piety, and gaiety. There is much symbolism attached, the teacher-pupil relationship being part of this. Remember, though, that the majority of Hindus belong to the Sudra caste or are the so-called casteless "untouchables," and these are effectively removed from any respectable position within Hindu religious hierarchy through the lack of this exclusive initiation. These castes may have their own gurus.

Before marriage, the season of studenthood, initiated through the above mentioned ceremony, is culminated through another ritual announcing to the world that the young adult is ready to assume marital responsibilities.

Hindus cremate their dead, although castes here and there may adopt burial as their preferred funeral rite. A Brahman looks at cremation as a last sacrifice in which his body is offered to the gods; with this presentation the dead person allegedly assumes a new existence along with his ancestors. The role of rebirth is not made clear in the earliest sacred texts, but rebirth *is* expected, depending specifically upon the quality of karma of the dead individual.

There is also another type of initiation, called *deeksha*, which refers to the consecration of individuals for various functions or initiation into sects. A guru gives *deeksha* to his disciple, consecrating him as a sanctified one; performing *deeksha* has become widespread and fashionable with the number of modern religious sects established by freewheeling gurus all over the world. *Deeksha* often involves the giving of a syllable or syllables by the guru to his disciple that the disciple is expected to guard as a secret mystery and recite to himself. Since a guru may have many disciples, even the guru may not remember the mysterious syllable or syllables he gave. The *deeksha* syllable(s) is/are believed to have an extraordinarily salvific role for the disciple.

FOUR STAGES IN LIFE

Hindus recognize four types of *ashrama*, or lifestyle, relating to the religious life of the individual: student, householder, forest hermit, and renouncer. Originally, each of these lifestyles was considered to be a permanent pursuit of an individual; that is, an individual would choose to be a Vedic student, a householder, a forest hermit, or a renouncer for his whole life. However, over time these four avocations became the four *stages* in the life of an individual. An upper-caste man thus starts his life as a student, and eventually he gets married. When he is at an appropriate age, with grandchildren and family well settled, his hair turning gray and his skin wrinkling, he will choose to go to the forest to live as a hermit for a period of time and meditate. Then at some point he will give up this stage as well, renounce his life completely, and become a nameless person—no roots, no family relationships. Renunciation is supposed to help liberate the soul from the unending cycle of births and deaths.

This fourfold lifestyle system (and the fourfold caste system) became the basis of all Hindu belief and practice, at least for the upper castes. This is an ideal that attracts people as a grand concept, both among Hindus and among Westerners seeking some novel experience. In reality, it is not practiced on a large scale; however, it is deeply ingrained in every devout Hindu as a goal worth pursuing.

WOMEN AND LOWER CASTES EXCLUDED FROM RITUALS

Hindu women are not usually allowed to undergo the initiation ritual, and they are forbidden to study the Veda, although rituals connected with childhood, marriage, pregnancy, and childbirth are performed for them. Marriage is the ritual of initiation for women. The place of the woman in traditional Hindu society is assured through the place of her father, husband, or her protector brother or son. She does not follow any of the four lifestyle stages (student, householder, forest hermit, and renouncer) on her own.

The Sudras and the fifth category of casteless people are not allowed to recite or even to hear the recitation of the Vedic texts, according to tradition. However, many of these communities have invented their own initiation ceremonies. (Pursuit of the elite is the goal of the downtrodden in every society.) The dominant role played by the upper castes in the social, economic, and cultural life of the Hindu allowed some freedom to the other castes to devise their own religious fulfillment so long as these efforts were not in conflict with the interests of the upper castes.

IMPORTANCE OF RITUALS

What distinguishes a ritual Hindu from other types of Hindus is his firm belief that it is through the performance of the prescribed rituals that the universe is sustained. Rituals are directed to personal and social ends—fertility, harvest, longevity, prosperity—being seen as an important mode of transaction between the gods and humanity.

The rituals and sacrifices are closely related; it is through the ritual that the sacrifice becomes prominent. Brahmans and other ritual-minded Hindus recognize two major types of rituals: those that are performed on a regular basis throughout the year and the lifetime of the individual, and rituals that are performed in order to seek the fruition of the wishes of the doer of the ritual. A third category of the ritual is *prayashchitta*, which is performed to rectify the transgressions or blunders committed by the individual.

How Rituals Are Performed

Rituals are performed without emotion or stirring of the heart, often mechanically, with abundant caution that the performance should strictly adhere to the traditionally laid-out procedures. Hindus may perform rituals not only to benefit themselves and the society but also to harm others and bring havoc upon the adversarial society or family. Sacrifice may come in the form of offering cows, milk, dairy products, garments, or other material objects.

Different temples may have different procedures and sacrificial systems, but the temple authorities are zealous about preserving the sanctity and tradition of rituals. Rituals are usually performed by a *purohita* (pandit) or a number of *purohitas* who are hired for the purpose. These are carefully chosen because the sacred texts demand that they not only be from the Brahman families but they also should have no bodily defects, should have the skill to perform the ritual without any blunder, and should be able to recite the words correctly without any pronunciation error.

If an error is committed in the recitation or pronunciation of a mantra, the ritual may turn against the persons for whose benefit the same is being performed. In general, wrong recitation and/or pronunciation in the conduct of the ritual will result in the annihilation of the result of the sacrifice. People who have commissioned the *purohitas* to conduct the rituals and sacrifice are simply eyewitnesses to the performance; so the Brahman priest, through his mantra, becomes a mediator to entice or anger (depending on the purpose) the gods to act on behalf of the persons or family that has commissioned the ritual.

The focus is not on the gods but on the ritual and on how to accomplish things through the gods by way of fulfilling the wishes of the commissioning party. The ritual is always accompanied by the uttered word or mantra; it is not merely the bodily action or the sacrifice or the offering that matters. Again, if the word or mantra is not recited flawlessly, the accompanying bodily action, sacrifice, and offering may not make the entire effort efficacious.

Sanskrit sacred texts always announce that speech leads the sacrifice to the gods; the word or mantra directs the ritual to its goal. The recitation of the mantra adopts several modulations of the voice: low, loud, moderate, or with frequent stopping. If the verses recited consist of more hard consonants, then the result would be different from those verses that consist of more soft consonants. Wishes dominate the rituals—prayer in the sense of moving the heart and soul of the worshiper as well as the Supreme Being is not a major part of the ritual's intent.

The *performers* of the rituals, the priests, have lost some social prestige even among the ritual Hindus because of their rather low economic status. However, the *performance* of rituals is gaining greater prestige and demand—there is a yearning in the hearts and minds of devout Hindus to go back to the original Vedic models of worship, ritual, and sacrifice.

There are hundreds of thousands of Hindu temples in India and neighboring countries manned by hundreds of thousands of priests, both from the Brahman and non-Brahman communities. Generally speaking, the non-Brahman priests are not trained in Sanskrit verses.

WHY ARE RITUALS ATTRACTIVE?

As already pointed out, ritualism is the backbone of Hinduism, so your Hindu friends will do their best to explain to you the importance of their ritual practices. Many will try to justify these rituals based on certain "scientific" facts; since science is the ruling "deity" of our modern secular civilization, Hindus seek justification for their practices based on scientific precepts.

A second attractive quality of Hindu rituals is that many of these are organized in tune with ideals that may sound intriguing and exciting. Each step in the ritual is given an explanation in high-sounding words; for example, a modern person experiencing strain and stress because of the frantic pace of modern life yearns to leave his world and seek peace elsewhere. The four stages of life suggested in Hinduism—student, householder, forest hermit, and renouncer—attract the attention of adventurous minds seeking to get away from it all.

The focus on the futility of life in general is a great attraction to disturbed souls.

A third attraction to Hindu rituals is that they always have some element of magic to them. Much power is vested in the words, or the mantras. The rigorous discipline and flawless pronunciation and strict adherence to the procedures further enhance the supposed value of the words uttered. This gives a sense of being in control of everything, including the gods. The performer of the ritual, as well as the supporter for whom the ritual is being performed, becomes the master of his own pursuits in this arrangement.

Fourth in the list of ways Hindu rituals attract adherents is the sanctity that is derived from an understanding that the rituals have been performed with very little alteration throughout the ages. It is truly a timeless exercise, so the devout Hindu thinks. The gods have long been manipulated to fend for the needs of humans. One may ask how Hinduism continues to survive in the face of Islam and Christianity. The fundamentalists among Hindus would say they have survived mainly because they continue to adhere to the rituals despite adversity.

WHY DO RITUALS NOT SAVE?

It is important that we convey to our Hindu friends that worship of God must be done in spirit and in truth. True spiritual worship does not consist of form or procedure but focuses only on the glory of God: we praise Him and thank Him for who He is. Spiritual worship is not manipulation of God but rather seeking His guidance and enjoying His presence. It does not need any ornamental arrangement but only a clean heart and a contrite spirit. True worship focuses on God alone, who is all truth and light—there is no darkness in Him. He is supportive of our being, but He is not supportive of our whims and fancies when these go against His will. He cannot be expected to take our side when we make evil plans.

We worship God in truth when we worship Him alone, to the exclusion of all other gods. There is no god other than the living God, the Creator of heaven and earth. The "gods" of this world are spiritual beings bent on misleading us. They may have special powers, but their character is not flawless. Their life histories narrated in the stories of religious texts and other mythologies reveal that their character is as deficient as fallen human nature. Worshiping these gods is not worshiping God in truth.

Hindus generally recognize character deficits in many of their gods. But in their view the world of the gods is similar to the world of humanity, and they do not expect anything more. Most of them do not realize that character flaws and social ills mainly spring from their blind acceptance of the model or models provided by their gods. While their heart tells them that something is wrong, even evil, with their behavior, they can easily find justification for it because their gods have performed the same acts under similar conditions. For the vast majority of Hindus, the gods cannot be questioned or faulted by mere humans, even though Hindu mythology narrates stories in which devout persons question the correctness of the position or acts of the gods and are sometimes victorious over them on the moral plane with the help of more superior powers, such as Fate.

If a Hindu friend at any time highlights the ritual that he follows or adheres to, an opening is provided for you to discuss this issue. The ministry of Jesus is full of instances in which He stood against ritualism. Although there are several dissimilarities between the Pharisees and the Hindu *purohitas*, the similarities in their attitudes toward religious matters and life in general are astounding. The Word of God rebukes ritualism in both the Old and New Testaments.

Consider the following quotations from Isaiah and Amos:

> "The multitude of your sacrifices—what are they to me?" says the LORD. "I have more than enough of burnt offerings, of rams and the fat of fattened animals; I have no pleasure in the blood of bulls and lambs and goats. When you come to appear before me, who has asked this of you, this trampling of my courts? Stop bringing meaningless offerings! Your incense is detestable to me. New Moons, Sabbaths and convocations—I cannot bear your evil assemblies. Your New Moon festivals and your appointed feasts my soul hates. They have become a burden to me; I am weary of bearing them. When you spread out your hands in prayer, I will hide my eyes from you; even if you offer many prayers, I will not listen. Your hands are full of blood" (Isaiah 1:11–15).
>
> "I hate, I despise your religious feasts; I cannot stand your assemblies. Even though you bring me burnt offerings and grain offerings, I will not accept them. Though you bring

choice fellowship offerings, I will have no regard for them. Away with the noise of your songs! I will not listen to the music of your harps" (Amos 5:21–23).

The Pharisees of the New Testament and the ritual Hindu priests have done their utmost to serve their respective religions. The Word of God, though, sees in them also the negativism developed through traditions.

> For I tell you that unless your righteousness surpasses that of the Pharisees and the teachers of the law, you will certainly not enter the kingdom of heaven. (Matthew 5:20)
> Then Jesus said to the crowds and to his disciples: "The teachers of the law and the Pharisees sit in Moses' seat. So you must obey them and do everything they tell you. But do not do what they do, for they do not practice what they preach. They tie up heavy loads and put them on men's shoulders, but they themselves are not willing to lift a finger to move them. Everything they do is done for men to see: They make their phylacteries wide and the tassels on their garments long; they love the place of honor at banquets and the most important seats in the synagogues; they love to be greeted in the market-places and to have men call them 'Rabbi' " (Matthew 23: 1–7).

The Pharisees held themselves aloof from the rest of the world through assiduous cultivation and observance of rituals. They were devoted to their religiosity, but the fulfillment of religion, for them, was only through the performance of rituals and strict adherence to the traditions. The apostle Paul says that they judged people according to the Law of Moses while they themselves did not follow it. Legalism dominated their way of life; they were hypocrites. They built tombs for the prophets and decorated the graves of the righteous, but they did not follow the counsel of the prophets. Moreover, they took joy in getting rid of the prophets while the prophets were alive because the prophets were critical of legalism (Matthew 23:29–31). They were like "whitewashed tombs, which look beautiful on the outside but on the inside are full of dead men's bones and everything unclean. In the same way, on the outside you [the Pharisees] appear to people as righteous but on the inside you are full of hypocrisy and wickedness" (Matthew 23:27–28).

"Once, having been asked by the Pharisees when the kingdom of God would come, Jesus replied, 'The kingdom of God does not come with your careful observation, nor will people say, "Here it is," or "There it is," because the kingdom of God is within you' " (Luke 17:20–21).

The Pharisees worked hard to propagate their religion, but once they gained a convert, they made him a greater slave to legalism. Jesus said,

> You travel over land and sea to win a single convert, and when he becomes one, you make him twice as much a son of hell as you are. Woe to you, blind guides! You say, "If anyone swears by the temple, it means nothing; but if anyone swears by the gold of the temple, he is bound by his oath." You blind fools! Which is greater: the gold, or the temple that makes the gold sacred? You also say, "If anyone swears by the altar, it means nothing; but if anyone swears by the gift on it, he is bound by his oath." You blind men! Which is greater: the gift, or the altar that makes the gift sacred? Therefore, he who swears by the altar swears by it and by everything on it. And he who swears by the temple swears by it and by the one who dwells in it. And he who swears by heaven swears by God's throne and by the one who sits on it. Woe to you, teachers of the law and Pharisees, you hypocrites! You give a tenth of your spices—mint, dill and cummin. But you have neglected the more important matters of the law—justice, mercy and faithfulness. You should have practiced the latter, without neglecting the former. You blind guides! You strain out a gnat but swallow a camel. (Matthew 23:15–24)

The problem with ritualism is that it focuses on the external and loses the spirit. It enslaves people, and those who focus on rituals alone as the method of worship lose their freedom. Jesus said that if we know truth, the truth will set us *free* (John 8:32); it is for *freedom* that Christ has set us free (Galatians 5:1).

Ritualism is also exhibitionism, which God detests in one's prayer life: "When you pray, do not be like the hypocrites, for they love to pray standing in the synagogues and on the street corners to be seen by men. I tell you the truth, they have received their reward in full" (Matthew 6:5).

One of the most telling passages in the Bible regarding the futility and irrelevance of ritualism is found in Matthew 12:

> At that time Jesus went through the grainfields on the Sabbath. His disciples were hungry and began to pick some heads of grain and eat them. When the Pharisees saw this, they said to him, "Look! Your disciples are doing what is unlawful on the Sabbath." He answered, "Haven't you read what David did when he and his companions were hungry? He entered the house of God, and he and his companions ate the consecrated bread—which was not lawful for them to do, but only for the priests. Or haven't you read in the Law that on the Sabbath the priests in the temple desecrate the day and yet are innocent? I tell you that one greater than the temple is here. If you had known what these words mean, 'I desire mercy, not sacrifice,' you would not have condemned the innocent. For the Son of Man is Lord of the Sabbath." Going on from that place, he went into their synagogue, and a man with a shriveled hand was there. Looking for a reason to accuse Jesus, they asked him, "Is it lawful to heal on the Sabbath?" He said to them, "If any of you has a sheep and it falls into a pit on the Sabbath, will you not take hold of it and lift it out? How much more valuable is a man than a sheep! Therefore it is lawful to do good on the Sabbath" (vv. 1–12).

Hindus recognize that ritualism can be a deterrent to doing good. There are stories involving Hindu saints and mythical characters that speak of the need to lay aside the rituals and acknowledge the value of men even if they are from lowly castes. There are also stories that show the gods did not care for the rituals, and how they came out to help people. However, such stress on doing away with rituals and seeking truth and goodness is not woven into the dominant worldview of Hinduism. Since it is believed the gods desire worship through rituals, and since the rituals are believed to have inherent power independent of the powers of the gods, performing rituals becomes an end in itself.

It is important to remember that Hinduism and ritualism go hand in hand. Most Hindus see their religion in operation mainly through the performance of rituals. Discussing the relevance of rituals and showing how futile it is to seek God through them will be better received by ritual Hindu friends later in your dialogue and relationship with them.

When the time seems right, allow your Hindu friend to tell you what significance the rituals he practices have for him. You can raise several questions about how and if these rituals contribute to any spiritual experience of God for him: What is the relevance of having the rituals performed through the offices of priests as intermediaries? Does your friend believe significant spiritual life is possible through rituals that demand more mechanical performance than spiritual participation? Does he know and understand the meaning of the verses he recites? Does he believe in what he recites? Or is it simply tradition that forces him to perform these rituals? Is it a desire to be distinct from the "lower" classes that motivates him? Why are women not allowed to be full participants? Does he think the gods that are the focus of the rituals worthy of worship? Do they display perfect or even good character?

You may become weary of listening to the claims of the relevance of these rituals, but be patient. Logical reasoning alone will not help remove the age-old dominance of ritualism in the heart and practice of your Hindu friend. While secularism has helped to some extent to blunt the support for rituals among Hindus, there is great revivalism going on in those communities that have traditionally performed and supported ritual Hinduism. At the same time, scholarly interest in ritual Hinduism among the students of Hindu civilization in Western nations has helped revive the prestige and pride of ritual Hinduism.

You could share how Jesus taught us to focus more on truth and simple, direct worship and prayer than on rituals, even though the Jews throughout history have resented the New Testament verses on the Pharisees and their observance of rituals as anti-Semitic. A criticism of the ritual approach to worship and prayer is often taken as an attack on the class of persons that performs such rituals. A critical analysis of the rituals performed by Hindus is often considered an attack on the Hindu religion and the priestly caste. For this reason, we must be cautious, thoughtful, gentle, and loving when approaching the subject.

CHAPTER

INTELLECTUAL HINDUS

3

Contrary to common belief, scriptural Hinduism is an intellectually oriented belief system. While the religion itself cannot be easily described because of so many different streams of tradition, the philosophical bases of Hinduism are very strong.

As previously stated, the majority of Hindus practice what we may call folk religion, having little or no acquaintance with their sacred texts. The temple sculptures and the mythologies they hear being narrated in public functions or from their elders have been the prime method of instruction for these Hindus. Traditionally, Hindu society is not literate, although Hindu civilization has always viewed literacy as an important and highly valued skill. Remember that Sanskrit, the language that embodies most of the Hindu scriptures, was not supposed to be taught to or learned by the lower castes, which form the majority.

Yet a significant section among the Hindus, especially from the upper castes (Brahmans, Kshatriyas, and Vaisyas), has always been engaged in spiritual inquiries. The four sacred texts, called *Vedas* (meaning sacred knowledge)—Rig-veda, Sama-veda, Yajur-veda, and Atharva-veda—are the earliest hymn-like compilations, dedications, prayers, litanies, rhythmic chants, charms, incantations, and spells composed by various authors. Each Veda consists of four constituents: the original text, guides for the proper ritual of hymns and prayers, performance of ritual sacrifices by those who left the community and went into the forest to pursue secluded religious life and meditation, and dialogues and discussions between a teacher and his disciples on the theme of ultimate wisdom. By far the most important segment of the sacred texts for the development of intellectual Hinduism is the fourth category, called *Upanishads,* written probably between 800 and 600 B.C. More than any other part of the four Vedas, the Upanishads continue to have the greatest impact on the Hindu educated classes. Often, the intellectual Hindus draw solace and inspiration from them in times of crisis, and they seek an identity of their wisdom and understanding with those of the Upanishads, which were composed by all classes of people, not only by the members of the Brahman communities.

Modern political and religious movements among the Hindus have often tended to draw their sustenance from their perception of the contents of the Vedas. A person educated in "vedic ideals" is often a tolerant universalist, accepting the caste divisions (barely mentioned in the Vedas) and insisting on the protection of the cow, although meat-eating and cow sacrifice were common in vedic times.

The Upanishads inaugurated a change in the direction of Hinduism. In the early vedic period, the focus was on *sacrifices* to the gods to keep them happy and benevolent. Upanishads moved toward *asceticism* as the valuable basis of religion. Worldly activities were looked down upon and people were encouraged to look inward and to develop a spiritual inclination beyond sacrifice and ritual. Also, one of the most important Hindu beliefs, that every man is a part of god or Paramaatman (Universal Soul), was firmly established by the Upanishadic teaching.

Subsequently, the immortality of the soul was accepted, and two kinds of souls—the Supreme Universal Soul (Paramaatman) and the personal individual soul of a living being (jeevaatman)—were distinguished. It was believed that the union of soul and body is bondage and causes misery to humans, so the goal was to abandon the body and free the soul from its ignorance that the Supreme Being and the individual soul are distinct. Separation from the Supreme Being, then, is wrong. A complete union with the Universal Soul (Paramaatman) achieves salvation or liberation—*moksha.*

Liberation from bondage is possible only through abstaining from every type of action, for action leads to likes and dislikes that add to attachment to one's action and possessions that, in turn, leads to the strengthening of the bondage. Because the soul is not detached from the body, an unending cycle of births and rebirths results. This is the basic scheme of reasoning among the intellectual Hindus and is interpreted in several ways through various schools of thought among Hindu savants.

KARMA—THE CONSEQUENCE OF DEEDS

Karma is an important and peculiar Hindu concept, although Buddhism shares aspects of karma, with some modification. (A major difference between karma followed in Hinduism and karma followed in Buddhism is that in the former, karma is closely linked to the caste system practiced by the Hindus, according to which a person may be born in a low or upper caste as a consequence of his karma. On the other hand, Buddhism does not posit any caste relation for karma.) Karma means *deeds* or *acts* or *works*. One's thoughts, words, and works in this life have a consequence in the next life, regulating what someone is in social station. Emotions that one experiences in this life are a result of what that person did in his previous life. Karma, then, results in appropriate reward or punishment in the future.

> *Karma* is a principle of moral reaction applied to both good and evil actions. As a man sows, so shall he reap. Bad actions reap suffering and bondage to human existence. Good actions lead to freedom from this bondage. . . . According to Karmic law, a man may be reborn as a god, as a member of a higher or lower caste, or as an animal, according to his every thought, word, and act. Each man, therefore, carries with him his past; in fact, he is his own past. . . . Similarly the mental and moral tendencies of this life will work themselves out in the next . . . the state of each creature in any particular life being dependent on the good or evil actions of preceding lives. (Nicholls, 142–43 [see bibliography for this and other references])

The results of karma cannot be avoided or overcome by any other means—even the gods cannot help a person to overcome its consequences. Karma has been a convenient justification for the poverty and low social status of millions of Hindus; it is also a clever way of protecting and sustaining the interests of the upper castes, especially the Brahmans, because of its religious promise that a lower-caste person will have a chance to improve his lot in his next birth if he accepts what is ordained for him now. Consequently, karma extends the perpetuation of discrimination.

Apart from its support to the caste institution, karma (in an indirect way) also glorifies good works as a source of liberation from the unending cycle of birth, death, and rebirth. Karma is used to explain all suffering: If a person is born deformed, it is because of karma in his past life; if a person wants to have happiness in a future life, he must work for it right now, regardless of the situation in which he is placed. He must suffer for his acts of commission and omission; there is no such concept as forgiveness, so he must achieve his salvation through his own efforts.

Unfortunately, we all know that no human being can ever be perfect, and that all of us will commit sin in our life in our thinking, speech, and actions. No amount of hard work and conscious effort can save us from committing sin. Although the principle may be an enticing one for intellectually oriented skeptics of Christ, it is totally flawed. Works alone cannot save a person.

THE PLACE OF WORKS IN THE PLAN OF SALVATION

God certainly wants us to do good works. He, in fact, helps us and blesses us as we do them: "Let your light shine before men, that they may see your good deeds and praise your Father in heaven" (Matthew 5:16). "For we are God's workmanship, created in Christ Jesus to do good works, which God prepared in advance for us to do" (Ephesians 2:10).

Jesus himself is an example: "God anointed Jesus of Nazareth with the Holy Spirit and power, and . . . he went around doing good and healing all who were under the power of the devil, because God was with him" (Acts 10:38).

The Bible says that God remembers good works: "God is not unjust; he will not forget your work and the love you have shown him as you have helped his people and continue to help them" (Hebrews 6:10).

It is clearly said, "We must all appear before the judgment seat of Christ, that each one may receive what is due him for the things done while in the body, whether good or bad" (2 Corinthians 5:10).

We are commanded:

> Be careful not to do your "acts of righteousness" before men, to be seen by them. If you do, you will have no reward from your Father in heaven. . . . But when you give to the

needy, do not let your left hand know what your right hand is doing, so that your giving may be in secret. Then your Father, who sees what is done in secret, will reward you. (Matthew 6:1–4)

May our Lord Jesus Christ himself and God our Father, who loved us and by his grace gave us eternal encouragement and good hope, encourage your hearts and strengthen you in every good deed and word. (2 Thessalonians 2:16–17)

In a large house there are articles not only of gold and silver, but also of wood and clay; some are for noble purposes and some for ignoble. If a man cleanses himself from the latter, he will be an instrument for noble purposes, made holy, useful to the Master and prepared to do any good work. (2 Timothy 2:20–21)

At one time we too were foolish, disobedient, deceived and enslaved by all kinds of passions and pleasures. We lived in malice and envy, being hated and hating one another. But when the kindness and love of God our Savior appeared, he saved us, not because of righteous things we had done, but because of his mercy. He saved us through the washing of rebirth and renewal by the Holy Spirit, whom he poured out on us generously through Jesus Christ our Savior, so that, having been justified by his grace, we might become heirs having the hope of eternal life. This is a trustworthy saying. And I want you to stress these things, so that those who have trusted in God may be careful to devote themselves to doing what is good. These things are excellent and profitable for everyone. (Titus 3:3–8)

"Yes," says the Spirit, "they will rest from their labor, for their deeds will follow them" (Revelation 14:13).

THE INSUFFICIENCY OF WORKS FOR SALVATION

God has asked us to do good works toward each other and live a sanctified life. He has assured us that all our good works will be rewarded. Although it is said that we will receive the suitable punishment for evil deeds that are unconfessed, God is merciful and gracious. He wants us to repent of our sins and put our trust in Him, not in our works. If we do this, He will save us. However, doing good works does not lead to the salvation of an individual; neither does it ensure a better life in the future. Good works are thoroughly insufficient for our salvation; it is God who redeems our life from the grave (Psalm 49:15).

No man can redeem the life of another or give to God a ransom for him—the ransom for a life is costly, no payment is ever enough—that he should live on forever and not see decay. (Psalm 49:7–9)

Unless the LORD builds the house, its builders labor in vain. Unless the LORD watches over the city, the watchmen stand guard in vain. In vain you rise early and stay up late, toiling for food to eat—for he grants sleep to those he loves. (Psalm 127:1–2)

All of us have become like one who is unclean, and all our righteous acts are like filthy rags; we all shrivel up like a leaf, and like the wind our sins sweep us away. (Isaiah 64:6)

I will expose your righteousness and your works, and they will not benefit you. (Isaiah 57:12)

Therefore, son of man, say to your countrymen, "The righteousness of the righteous man will not save him when he disobeys, and the wickedness of the wicked man will not cause him to fall when he turns from it. The righteous man, if he sins, will not be allowed to live because of his former righteousness." If I tell the righteous man that he will surely live, but then he trusts in his righteousness and does evil, none of the righteous things he has done will be remembered; he will die for the evil he has done. And if I say to the wicked man, "You will surely die," but he then turns away from his sin and does what is just and right—if he gives back what he took in pledge for a loan, returns what he has stolen, follows the decrees that give life, and does no evil, he will surely live; he will not die. None of the sins he has committed will be remembered against him. He has done what is just and right; he will surely live. (Ezekiel 33:12–16)

To some who were confident of their own righteousness and looked down on everybody else, Jesus told this parable: "Two men went up to the temple to pray, one a Pharisee and the other a tax collector. The Pharisee stood up and prayed about himself: 'God, I thank you that I am not like other men—robbers, evildoers, adulterers—or even like this tax collector. I fast twice a week and give a tenth of all I get.' But the tax collector stood at a distance. He would not even look up to heaven, but beat his breast and said, 'God, have mercy on me, a sinner.' I tell you that this man, rather than the other, went home justified before God. For everyone who exalts himself will be humbled, and he who humbles himself will be exalted" (Luke 18:9–14).

Therefore, my brothers, I want you to know that through Jesus the forgiveness of sins is proclaimed to you. Through him everyone who believes is justified from everything you could not be justified from by the law of Moses. (Acts 13: 38–39)

What then shall we say that Abraham, our forefather, discovered in this matter? If, in fact, Abraham was justified by works, he had something to boast about—but not before God. What does the Scripture say? "Abraham believed God, and it was credited to him as righteousness" (Romans 4:1–3).

It does not, therefore, depend on man's desire or effort, but on God's mercy. (Romans 9:16)

If by grace, then it is no longer by works; if it were, grace would no longer be grace. (Romans 11:6)

A man is not justified by observing the law, but by faith in Jesus Christ. (Galatians 2:16)

For it is by grace you have been saved, through faith—and this not from yourselves, it is the gift of God—not by works, so that no one can boast. (Ephesians 2:8–9)

SOCIAL DIVISION IN HINDUISM—CASTES

As we stated in the beginning, a Hindu is characterized by his belief in at least three principles: acceptance and practice of the caste system, belief in transmigration of souls (samsara—see below), and karma.

Again, the Code of Manu, written perhaps in the fifth century B.C., classified Hindu society as consisting of four primary social divisions (castes) in the following descending order of rank: *Brahman*, the priestly class; *Kshatriya*, the military class; *Vaisya*, the agriculturist and business class; and *Sudra*, the servant class.

"From priority of birth, from superiority of origin (in being sprung from the mouth of the Creator), from possession of the Veda (i.e., from the right of repeating, teaching, and expounding it), and from a distinction in the reception of the sacrificial thread" (Monier-Williams, 57), the Brahmans were considered to be the head of all classes. The result of the Code of Manu was that it put the Brahman

above everyone else and made him the controller and chief benefici-
ary of the system. Another pernicious and destructive consequence
was the notion of the *untouchables* or polluted classes. Those who
were required to perform "unclean" jobs were given very few or no
civil rights.

The caste system has been criticized as discriminatory and retro-
grade by the social reformers among Hindus. But without the caste
system, Hinduism is not Hinduism. By birth, man's station in life is
fixed; what he should do and what he should not do, what he should
aspire to become and what he should not aspire to become is all
decided by the caste into which he is born. If he is born into a Brahman caste, he is a Brahman, and he will have access to his Vedas and
all the privileges that go with it. If he is born into the soldiers' caste,
he is expected to pursue only that profession as his forefathers willingly did. Caste is an institution into which he is born, and he will
continue to be a part of it until he dies; one may change his religion,
but not his caste. Nearly 20 percent of the current Hindu population
belongs to the category of "untouchables," with whom any physical
contact is prohibited. Even the shadow of an untouchable is *traditionally* treated as causing ritual pollution.

With the advent of British rule and the continuous efforts of missionaries, untouchability as a public, social phenomenon began to be
resented by many, but not all, Western-educated Hindus. Although
law abolishes this social evil, and although there is very severe punishment meted out to those who practice it in public places, several
groups of orthodox Hindus and their religious leaders still try to justify it.

As John Noss (108) points out,

> When the caste system was linked up with the Law of
> Karma, the inequalities of life had at once a simple and com-
> prehensive explanation. The existence of caste in the social
> structure immediately acquired a kind of moral justification. If
> a man was born a Shudra [Sudra], it was because he had
> sinned in previous existences and deserved no better lot. A
> Brahman, on the other hand, had every right to exalt his posi-
> tion and prerogatives; by good deeds in previous existence he
> had merited his present high station. The social consequences
> of the moral justification of caste were apparent in another
> direction. Any attempt to level up the inequalities of society

and to lay broader basis for social justice and reward now became either impious or morally wrong-headed. To question the operations of the Law of Karma as fitting the just retribution for deeds in former lives became the rankest of heresies.

It is no wonder, then, that the gospel proclamation that Jesus came to save the poor and the lowly has begun to strike a sympathetic chord in the hearts of the lower castes and the so-called untouchable communities among the Hindus.

Both secular and religious Hindu intellectuals have generally acknowledged the evil effects of the caste system, but they appreciate and cling to the principle of karma as a positive tenet of Hinduism. The general tendency among upper-caste Hindus and political leaders is to retain the caste system but do their best to eliminate its evil effects. They seem to separate karma from the damaging side of the caste system and retain it as a regulatory code for the Hindu way of life. They justify the concept and the rule of karma through simple but unsound metaphors or analogies, and they focus upon the freedom of choice given to the soul while glossing over the heavy baggage it has to carry because of karmic predetermination. For example, "D. S. Sharma compares the soul to a farmer to whom a plot of land has been given. Its size, the nature of its soil, and weather conditions are predetermined; but the farmer is at liberty either to till the ground and raise crops, or to neglect it and allow it to run to waste" (Nicholls, 143).

On the other hand, S. Radhakrishnan, a well-known philosopher and former president of India, compared the operation of the karmic principle to that of a card game: "The cards in the game of life are given to us. We do not select them. They are traced to our past karma, but we can call as we please, lead what suit we will, and as we play, we gain or lose. And there is freedom" (Ibid.).

THE PROBLEM OF CASTE

This focus on freedom of choice, on the glorification of self-help, and on rugged individualism at the theoretical level, without considering for a moment how karma in reality has been used as a diabolical tool to oppress and exploit people, has led to its easy marketability and wide acceptance in the thoughts of secular Western man. Since Western man is not subjected to such oppression in his own society at present, he looks at karma only as a psychosomatic tool. In fact, it bloats his ego in several ways because he thinks that his karma must have been good in order for him to have such a comfortable life.

Generally speaking, even Indian Christians, especially those hailing from southern India, have not given up their caste status; for instance, they tend to marry only within them. In the past the church, both Catholic and Protestant, tried to eliminate caste affiliations among converts from Hinduism. At times the policy of accommodation was also adopted, and this encouraged the growth of caste feelings and affiliations within the Christian community to the detriment of the growth of the church. Everyone pays lip service to the demand that caste be eradicated, but caste affiliations continue to grow and have become a deciding factor in elections, employment, and every walk of life in India. There are Christian scholars both in India and Western nations who consider that caste may be treated as a bridge to reach out to various groups among the Hindus.

Mostly those belonging to the upper and middle castes among the Hindus practice intellectual Hinduism, in the sense of religion based on classical and sacred texts of Hinduism and attendant traditions. They tend to prefer to retain their caste and may not think that caste is an impediment to the progress of Hindu communities. They will often take the position that caste was originally a way established to categorize people based on their social and professional function. They may also acknowledge that there are some evil effects, but its original intent of situating people is still valid. Conversations with your Hindu friends will no doubt reveal their attitude toward the caste as an institution. Without attacking the caste institution, it is important for us to share what the Bible says about categorizing people. For example, an interesting model is found in what it says about the church as the body of Christ:

> The body is a unit, though it is made up of many parts; and though all its parts are many, they form one body. So it is with Christ. For we were all baptized by one Spirit into one body—whether Jews or Greeks, slave or free—and we were all given the one Spirit to drink. Now the body is not made up of one part but of many. If the foot should say, "Because I am not a hand, I do not belong to the body," it would not for that reason cease to be part of the body. And if the ear should

say, "Because I am not an eye, I do not belong to the body," it would not for that reason cease to be part of the body. If the whole body were an eye, where would the sense of hearing be? If the whole body were an ear, where would the sense of smell be? But in fact God has arranged the parts in the body, every one of them, just as he wanted them to be. If they were all one part, where would the body be? As it is, there are many parts, but one body. The eye cannot say to the hand, "I don't need you!" And the head cannot say to the feet, "I don't need you!" On the contrary, those parts of the body that seem to be weaker are indispensable, and the parts that we think are less honorable we treat with special honor. And the parts that are unpresentable are treated with special modesty, while our presentable parts need no special treatment. But God has combined the members of the body and has given greater honor to the parts that lacked it, so that there should be no division in the body, but that its parts should have equal concern for each other. If one part suffers, every part suffers with it; if one part is honored, every part rejoices with it. (1 Corinthians 12:12–26)

To treat people as subhumans is not acceptable according to the Word of God. The Bible says that we are all created in His image (Genesis 1:26–27; 5:1, 3; 9:6; 1 Corinthians 11:7; Colossians 3:10; James 3:9). If we are all created as such, what justification do we have for discriminating against people based on birth?

"The most important [command]," answered Jesus, "is this: 'Hear, O Israel, the Lord our God, the Lord is one. Love the Lord your God with all your heart and with all your soul and with all your mind and with all your strength.' The second is this: 'Love your neighbor as yourself.' There is no commandment greater than these" (Mark 12:29–31). We need to tell Hindu friends how important it is for us all to love one another and not to discriminate based on color, birth, or gender. If a theological belief supports such discrimination, it is important for us to review the belief and discard it.

God is not a respecter of persons.

Like water spilled on the ground, which cannot be recovered, so we must die. But God does not take away life; instead, he devises ways so that a banished person may not remain estranged from him. (2 Samuel 14:14)

God does not show favoritism. (Romans 2:11)

And masters, treat your slaves in the same way. Do not
threaten them, since you know that he who is both their Master and yours is in heaven, and there is no favoritism with him.
(Ephesians 6:9)

Anyone who does wrong will be repaid for his wrong, and
there is no favoritism. (Colossians 3:25)

Christ has called us into a community of believers as children of
God. Even as we seek our own salvation as individuals, we are called
upon to be a branch of the fruit-bearing Vine. We are also called upon
to preach the gospel to others and to lead them to salvation. Jesus
said that the command "Love your neighbor as yourself" is the heart-
beat of all the law. The determination of one's place in life by his or
her birth, and the teaching that what one has now is a consequence
of what he or she did in previous lives, are all notions completely
unacceptable to Christ's teaching. If we love our neighbor, we have
no alternative but to reject the theological support lent by karma for
the institution of caste.

SAMSARA—THE TRANSMIGRATION OF SOULS IN ENDLESS REBIRTHS

Transmigration of souls, or reincarnation in endless rebirths, is a
cornerstone of Hindu belief. Souls are eternal, and they are reborn, it
is said, in new bodies. The soul does not die but is reborn into
another existence—rebirth follows rebirth until the chain or the cycle
is broken.

> The soul of a man who dies does not, except in the single
> case of one who at death returns into indistinguishable one-
> ness with *Brahman* (the Universal Soul), pass into a perma-
> nent state of being in heaven or hell or elsewhere; the soul,
> rather, is reborn into another existence that will terminate in
> due time and necessitate yet another birth. Rebirth follows
> rebirth, with the one exception named, in an endless chain.
> The successive births are not likely to be on the same plane of
> being. Rebirth may occur for a finite period of time in any of
> the series of heavens or hells, or upon earth in any of the forms
> of life, vegetable, animal, or human. It may thus be either
> higher or lower than the present or any past existence. (Noss,
> 106–107)

Hindus believe that the soul is not limited to humankind, but that plants, animals, and all living things share it. A dead person's soul may be born again in the body of any living thing. Thus, there is no guarantee that a human being will be reborn as a human being. Transmigration offers a progressive evolution from the lowest to the highest birth as a Brahman. There are, however, endless possibilities for backsliding in status. Man is involved in a game of chutes and ladders.

The ultimate goal is to obtain *moksha*, liberation from samsara, from the bondage of birth, death, and rebirth. Unfortunately, such liberation looks impossible because everyone commits some sin or another. Since there is no forgiveness provided, and since karma operates inexorably, anyone who commits any kind of sin is liable to suffer the consequence of his actions in his next life. For example, you are certain to be punished in your next life if your thought-life is sinful in this one. Even the smallest of all sins or errors would ensure that you have a rebirth and suffer the consequence of what you committed in your previous life. Thus there is no way any person can really get the much-desired liberation; only mythical characters may have obtained it. In the absence of the operation of forgiveness and mercy through grace, there is no way that any person can become saved within Hindu theology.

Because karma is unavoidable, and because one is bound to be reincarnated in some form after death and thus be ensured of a continuity of struggle, life is viewed as a dreary recycling of more suffering and pain. Hindu thought is often fatalistic because of the impact of karma and samsara. Although the success or release from the endless cycle of rebirths is to be achieved through self-help, fatalism works in exactly the opposite direction, discouraging every self-help effort due to the inevitable failure despite hard work.

Hindu literature and thinking is replete with the hope that what could not be achieved or is missed in this life may perhaps be attained in the next. A hopeful picture is drawn of tragic heroes of this life who rise high in their next rebirth and are given the comfort they sought in their earlier life. People may get another chance in their next life to improve their lot. This is an enticing opportunity, but unfortunately it is quite misleading. It justifies the present without enabling people to seek the forgiveness of God, whose Word plainly says that we have only one life and that we are judged after death based on what we do now (Hebrews 9:27). Since God is gracious, He *will* forgive our sins if we repent and make amends. It is our *faith* in Him that sanctifies us as worthy of His grace and forgiveness.

Once again, the writer of Hebrews makes it crystal clear that we have only one life, the present one: "Just as man is destined to die once, and after that to face judgment, so Christ was sacrificed once to take away the sins of many people" (Hebrews 9:27–28).

> We are confident, I say, and would prefer to be away from the body and at home with the Lord. So we make it our goal to please him, whether we are at home in the body or away from it. For we must all appear before the judgment seat of Christ, that each one may receive what is due him for the things done while in the body, whether good or bad. (2 Corinthians 5:8–10)
>
> I eagerly expect and hope that I will in no way be ashamed, but will have sufficient courage so that now as always Christ will be exalted in my body, whether by life or by death. For to me, to live is Christ and to die is gain. If I am to go on living in the body, this will mean fruitful labor for me. Yet what shall I choose? I do not know! (Philippians 1:20–22)

The story of the rich man and Lazarus (Luke 16:19–31) clearly mentions that those who have died are not born again into this world but are judged according to their deeds. Consider also Isaiah 14:9–11 and Revelation 20:11–15.

THE CONCEPT OF TRI-MURTI

Over the centuries Hindus have developed the notion of *Tri-murti*, the triad of divine forms. These three gods may be described as Creator, Preserver, and Destroyer: Brahma is the name given to the creator god, Vishnu is the name given to the preserver god, and Shiva is the name given to the destroyer god. It appears that the concept was an accommodation to several trends of thought, not excluding those of other races and tribal groups as well as Buddhists. Temples for Vishnu and Shiva are found everywhere in India, and these gods are worshiped regularly, but the temple for and worship of Brahma is a rarity.

Hindus sometimes confuse their Tri-murti and the Trinity; Christian Indians often try to communicate the concept of the Trinity using Tri-murti, which leads to the conception of Christianity as a polytheistic religion in the minds of Hindus. Some Hindu thinkers have claimed in the past that the three forms in Tri-murti constitute one god, but most texts treat these as three distinct divine beings. Each one has his own personality and mythology, not connected to each other in any essential spiritual sense—independent gods assigned different roles. For instance, Shiva is married and has his own children.

Devotees can choose to follow and worship any one of the three in preference to the other two. The gods of Hinduism indulge themselves in creation and other activities including participation and involvement in the lives of human beings as a sport (*leela*), or an amusement for themselves. They take the sides of humans in interpersonal conflicts, and such participation in the life of their devotees is not necessarily based on moral or ethical principles.

HINDU MYTHOLOGIES AND THEIR RELEVANCE FOR DAY-TO-DAY LIVING

Two great epics of the Hindus have influenced the masses as well as the intellectuals, providing them with models of exemplary behavior. First, *Ramayana* tells the story of Rama, one of the ten incarnations of Vishnu that is worshiped throughout India. While atheists and rationalists have criticized Rama's conduct as portrayed in the epic, Hindus themselves, especially in northern India, are very much devoted to his worship.

Second, *Mahabharata* is a long epic poem of the conflict between two related families, a collection of Hindu traditions, legendary history, ethics, and philosophy, all interwoven with the narrated story. From Mahabharata sprang many of the *puranas* (mythologies dealing with the incarnation of gods and their deliberations on earth), gods that get involved in the lives of men and other beings. Mahabharata and the puranas are the main source of religious knowledge for the Hindus, especially for those with little or no education. All draw their inspiration for morals and ethics from Ramayana and Mahabharata.

BHAGAVAD-GITA

Mahabharata has a long dialogue with Arjuna, the warrior prince, and his charioteer, Krishna, who is an incarnation of Vishnu. The dialogue is used as an opportunity to elucidate the important aspects of Hindu philosophy or worldview. This portion is called *Bhagavad-Gita*, meaning "song of the Lord." If Mahabharata and Ramayana influence the thinking patterns of all Hindus, both educated and uneducated, both belonging to the upper castes and the lower castes, Bhagavad-Gita has become the main staple food of thought for modern educated Hindus, whose numbers are swelling to greater proportions every year. In contemporary India, every Hindu thinks highly of Bhagavad-Gita, whether he has read it or not. Thus, if we wish to engage a Hindu in a conversation on spiritual matters, it becomes imperative that we know something about Bhagavad-Gita.

In the war between two closely related families, Krishna, who was related to both parties, refused to take up arms on either side but consented to act as the charioteer of Arjuna and to aid him with his advice.

> At the commencement of the Bhagavad-Gita, the two contending armies are supposed to be drawn up in battle-array, when Arjuna is struck with sudden compunction at the idea of fighting his way to a kingdom through the blood of his kindred, and asks Krishna's opinion as to his proper course of action. Krishna's reply is made the occasion of the long philosophical dialogue. . . . The main design of the poem . . . is to inculcate the doctrine of *bhakti*, (unconditional devotion), to exalt the duties of caste above all other obligations, including those of friendship and kindred. As Arjuna belongs to the military caste, he is exhorted to perform his appointed work as a soldier. Again and again is he urged to fight, without the least thought about consequences, and without the slightest question as to the propriety of slaughtering his relations. Hence we have the following sentiments often repeated:
>
> Better to do the duty of one's caste,
> Though bad and ill-performed and fraught with evil,
> Than undertake the business of another,
> However good it be. For better far
> Abandon life at once than not fulfill
> One's own appointed work; another's duty
> Brings danger to the man who meddles with it.
> Perfection is alone attained by him
> Who swerves not from the business of his caste. (Monier-Williams, 208)

Arjuna is comforted and encouraged to kill his relatives without distress because their soul is eternal, and nothing is destroyed. The duty before him, winning the war, and performing his ordained caste duty (*dharma*) are more important to follow. Hindus are encouraged to develop a worldview in what is ordained as the duty of their (social) position. It is more important than the doctrine "Love your neighbor as yourself." It is claimed that doing one's duty in a detached manner is the best form of worship. "Do your duty and do not worry about the consequence" is the mantra of the educated classes among the Hindus. Now it is being extended to perform civil duties in an objective way as ordained by the rules and regulations, even if it would cause immense harm. Such an approach leads to excessive harshness and violence and lacks empathy for the poor, needy, and suffering. On the other hand, the ideal within the Word of God is that love and mercy must go hand in hand with the performance of one's duties. Christ is seeking a relationship of love, and He wants us to do the same with our fellowman.

YOGA

It is Bhagavad-Gita that eulogized yoga as an instrument of moksha, or liberation from the bondage of births and rebirths. Modern Hinduism preaches yoga to people with a focus only on mental concentration, as a technique of getting peace and solace and good physical health. (It has become a fad in the West as an effective instrument to release one's tension.) Yoga is defined as "intense concentration of the mind on one subject [viz., The Supreme Being, here identified with Krishna], till at last the great end of freedom from all thought, perfect calm, and absorption in the Deity are obtained" (Monier-Williams, 210). Yoga is, indeed, a religious exercise that focuses upon obtaining oneness with deity. While it has several benefits as a physical exercise, the theology on which it is based and which it seeks to promote is counter to Christianity. In modern times, yoga is nicely stripped of its religious basis in several ways and is packaged and promoted as part of self-help spiritual tools for the culture.

DHARMA

The idea of dharma runs through every walk of life, and the greatest goal is to be an ardent follower and practitioner of it. Dharma certainly includes the way of life ordained for a caste that should be followed scrupulously by the individual if he wishes to improve his lot in future births. Dharma also is viewed as justice and righteousness and culture. In summary, each profession is viewed as having its own dharma, and the professional is expected to follow the ordained dharma of his profession.

SIN, SOUL, AND SALVATION IN HINDUISM

As we have already highlighted, the soul is thought of as eternal, and every being has its own soul, whether animal, human, or plant. This concept is closely connected to the samsara concept in which a man undergoes many rebirths before he is liberated from the bondage of the cycle of birth, death, and rebirth. Either the soul is individually eternal, or eternal in the Universal Soul through absorption

Liberation from the clutches of the body is the goal—the body becomes a "sinful" object. However, while the Christian knows the limitations of the body, he does not despise his body, because it is the temple of the Holy Spirit. Instead of seeking to discard the body altogether, he seeks a *new* spiritual body.

Sin in Hinduism is not considered to be personal moral guilt; rather, sin is the belief that attributes reality to this illusory world. Every interested action is sin, so Hinduism says to do your work without attachment to the consequences of action. For the sins of the body, you become an inanimate object in the next birth; for the sins of speech you become a bird in the next birth; for mental sins you will be born as a lower-caste person.

Christians, in contrast, view body and soul as a unity. Man is created in the image of God, with free will, rationality, and moral aspects.

THREE WAYS OF SALVATION

There are three supposed ways to attain salvation in Hinduism. *Karma marga* is the way of works, of performing caste duties scrupulously. Presently it is interpreted as doing your job or duties without attachment to the results. A parent's karma marga is doing the right thing in bringing up his children. An employee's karma marga is doing his duties truthfully.

Gnana marga is the way of knowledge. Using the intellect man has, he studies the Vedas and attains his wisdom from the sacred texts.

No emotion or relationship is involved.

Bhakti marga is the way of love and devotion to gods. Worshiping and praising the gods takes precedence over rituals or knowledge. It is not expected that any spiritual understanding is required to worship and praise the gods.

The way of works is the way of ritual. Rituals performed at home, in public places on special occasions, and in the temples on a regular basis all contribute to the merit of the individuals who either perform the rituals themselves or cause these rituals to be performed engaging the services of a purohita. Meticulous and unfailing performance of the rites and ceremonies appropriate to stages such as birth, marriage, harvest, or death adds to the merit of individuals.

Memorization and recitation of sacred verses as well as meditation on the Universal Soul through diligent study and inquiry helps one to recognize his own self and nature. This helps in the process of union with the Universal Soul (in the gnana marga).

Whereas only those who are intellectually oriented will choose the path of gnana marga, everyone who loves the gods can choose the bhakti marga as a way to salvation. All those who have no recourse to the other two ways of salvation generally adopt this way. These people often devote themselves to only one deity, chosen by the individual based on his inclination, and do not have much interest in self-examination or inclination toward great reasoning about spiritual matters. Hindu reformers have adopted bhakti marga as their message of salvation, preaching that bhakti or devotion to the gods eliminates caste disparities and unites people.

PROCESSES OF SALVATION

There are two processes of salvation identified by the philosophers, one called *cat-hold* and the other called *monkey-hold*. In cat-hold salvation, the deity carries the devotee with no effort at all on his part—he does not even cling to the deity. On the other hand, in monkey-hold, the deity does not mind the devotee clinging to him, but the deity itself does not make any effort to save the devotee. Like the young monkey clinging to its mother, who goes about doing her business, not caring about the baby, the devotee is to cling to the deity and goes with the deity wherever he goes. The former does not emphasize man's effort, while the latter does.

In our Christian belief, grace cancels the works of the law, and salvation is by the grace of the Lord. Since Hinduism accommodates everything into its theology, there *are* some schools of philosophy that hold to salvation by grace alone, teaching that grace hastens the process of deliverance from bondage to karma and samsara.

As we already pointed out, the Hindu god or gods operate within the bounds of karma. The Christian view of creation is that the universe is uniquely distinct from God and has a moral purpose; the Hindu view of creation is that god may transcend creation, but he is never entirely separated from it. According to the Hindu view, god continues creating as his play or sport (*leela*).

In modern times, Hinduism has found a close ally in the secular humanism of the West. Hindu apology (defense) aims at separating the Jesus of history from the Christ of faith, and it identifies Christian concepts with Hindu idealism, which in actuality was borrowed from the West. Since the tendency of Hindus is to see every idea in their religion, and since they deliberately seek to accommodate everything, they are unable to see the illusion they have created for themselves.

The three ways of salvation suggested in Hinduism are all based on works, attempts on the part of man to devise his own process of saving himself. We know that salvation by works is not possible, simply because no work will ever be perfect; unless there is grace, all our efforts toward salvation will be futile. It is important for us to emphasize this point to our Hindu friends: Without help and grace from God, salvation is impossible.

Jesus said, "All authority in heaven and on earth has been given to me. Therefore go and make disciples of all nations, baptizing them in the name of the Father and of the Son and of the Holy Spirit" (Matthew 28:18–19). There would have been no need for this command if Jesus believed that the religions of the world were the effective means of salvation for humankind.

Jesus also said, "The gospel must first be preached to all nations" (Mark 13:10). He commanded, "Go into all the world and preach the good news to all creation. Whoever believes and is baptized will be saved, but whoever does not believe will be condemned" (Mark 16:15–16). He added, "Repentance and forgiveness of sins will be preached in [my] name to all nations, beginning at Jerusalem" (Luke 24:47). In Acts 1:8, the disciples were told, "You will be my witnesses in Jerusalem, and in all Judea and Samaria, and to the ends of the earth." There would have been no need for these commands, either, if Jesus thought that the "news" these religions had was adequate enough for the salvation of humanity.

Jesus did not consider the law given to Moses as defective or deficient, for he declared, "Do not think that I have come to abolish the Law or the Prophets; I have not come to abolish them but to fulfill them" (Matthew 5:17). His manner of fulfilling the law, however, was revolutionary and upsetting for those who interpreted it differently than the way God intended.

Jesus clearly said, "I am the way and the truth and the life. No one comes to the Father except through me. If you really knew me, you would know my Father as well" (John 14:6–7). He also said, "Anyone who has seen me has seen the Father. How can you say, 'Show us the Father'? Don't you believe that I am in the Father and that the Father is in me? The words I say to you are not just my own. Rather, it is the Father, living in me, who is doing his work" (John 14:9–10).

THE CENTRALITY OF JESUS CHRIST

Following the Great Commission (Matthew 28:18–19; Mark 16:15–16), the apostle Paul writes, "Through him and for his name's sake, we received grace and apostleship to call people from among all the Gentiles to the obedience that comes from faith" (Romans 1:5). He also declared that he was not ashamed of the gospel, "because it is the power of God for the salvation of everyone who believes" (Romans 1:16).

The centrality of Jesus Christ in God's plan of salvation for humankind is clearly emphasized in the Bible. Paul writes, "If you confess with your mouth, 'Jesus is Lord,' and believe in your heart that God raised him from the dead, you will be saved" (Romans 10:9). He also asserts, "There is no difference between Jew and Gentile—the same Lord is Lord of all and richly blesses all who call on him, for, 'Everyone who calls on the name of the Lord will be saved' " (Romans 10:12–13).

With these and many more statements in the Bible, it seems futile for a practicing Christian to accept *any* claim that human salvation is possible through other religions that do not recognize the salvific role of Jesus Christ.

OTHER RELIGIONS: EXCHANGING THE GLORY OF GOD

"The wrath of God is being revealed against all the godlessness and wickedness of men," wrote Paul (Romans 1:18). Godlessness and wickedness are reflected in several ways, but one of the chief signs is exchanging "the glory of the immortal God for images made to look like mortal man and birds and animals and reptiles" (Romans 1:23). Paul was in agony when he saw humans trading the truth of God for a lie, worshiping and serving created things rather than the Creator (Romans 1:25).

Most Asian religions include idol worship in one form or another, and Hinduism is no exception, allowing the worship of the creature as creator. In addition to idols in different forms and shapes representing animals, humans, birds, reptiles, and so on, Hinduism allows its adherents to worship living beings as gods and spirits. Buddhism, which did not originally concern itself about God, has elevated its founder to the status of god. (Divination, sorcery, and spiritism also play an important role in the lives of Buddhists.)

Karma and samsara (transmigration of souls), the two crucial concepts of Hinduism and Buddhism, militate against the core of Christian belief. Confucianism, which totally ignored theology and focused on the proper manners of living, elevated Confucius to some sort of divinity. Also, ancestor worship, which revolves around the propitiation of ancestor spirits, cannot be justified within Christianity. Shinto likewise glorifies creation, not the Creator; living in harmony with nature takes precedence over the worship of God.

THE DIVINITY OF JESUS CHRIST—DENIED

These Eastern religions do not accept the divinity of Jesus Christ. Hindus may accept Jesus Christ as *one* of their gods, but not as God; neither do Buddhists and Shintoists see any reason to consider Jesus divine. Islam holds that Jesus was one of the prophets—sinless, but not superior to Muhammad. Associating Jesus with God is considered in Islam to be the gravest sin, from which no one can ever obtain pardon. For the Jew, Jesus may have been a rebel, albeit a well-meaning rebel, who was killed not because of them but because he rebelled against Rome. So wherever we turn, we see that other religions reject the exclusive divine status of Jesus Christ. However, affirmation and acknowledgment of "Jesus Christ as the unique and decisive revelation of God for the salvation of the world" is a prerequisite for salvation, according to the Bible.

CERTAIN IMPLICATIONS OF HINDU THEOLOGY

Belief in karma fosters belief in fate, so most Hindus are fatalistic in their attitude. Because of animism, pantheism, and polytheism, any object or person can become worthy of veneration and worship. Therefore, we find innumerable ascetics and gurus posing as divine men and women among Hindus, and a vast majority of Hindus are given to paying obeisance to such people for prosperity and the liberation of their souls. Because of their acceptance of karma, social exploitation and superstition are religiously sanctioned.

Due to polytheism, the exclusive salvific role of Christ is difficult for Hindus to accept. However, since Hindus are largely a group of people believing also in one Universal Supreme Being, they can grasp the meaning and significance of Yahweh God. Their question and problem concerns why they should give up their gods and accept Jesus as *the* Lord and Savior. Again, Hinduism is often equated with nationalism and patriotism.

The educated classes, especially those belonging to the Brahman castes, are prone to rationalization and justification of everything Hindu. They will acknowledge the sources of their modern ideals (which come largely from the Christian value system) but will assume that these are their own. For everything we suggest as Christian, they will claim to have the very same concept in their own religion. This identity may come from minor sources, which may be acknowledged but not highly valued or practiced, or such views may be part of a bigger system whose ultimate aim will be accommodation of pantheism and polytheism. More often than not, a Hindu sees only the similarity and inclusive features.

Remember that there is a wide gulf between the religion followed by the Brahmans and the religion followed by the vast majority of the non-Brahman castes. The intellectually worked-out design of Brahman Hinduism is not generally accessible to the masses, and the Brahmans look down upon the belief systems of the lower castes. Textual religious instruction of the lower castes is not attempted even now, while it was forbidden in the past. As mentioned before, the original sacred Hindu texts are in Sanskrit, no longer spoken as an ordinary language. The gulf between the prestigious upper castes and the less literate lower castes is bridged by religious literary stories—epics (Mahabharata and Ramayana) and various puranas (mythological stories) that abound in all kinds of deeds of the gods, which include indulging in moral, immoral, and amoral acts.

EVANGELIZING THE HINDUS

Christianity has spread mostly among the people of the lower social strata and among the tribal populations in India. As we have seen, according to Indian Christian tradition, the earliest Christian witness among the Hindus was the apostle Thomas, who was believed to have arrived in the first century and was martyred near Madras (now Chennai), a large city on the east coast of southern India.

The Syrian Rite Church has been in existence for at least twelve hundred years. It remained, however, ethnocentric, and the Syrian Christians evolved themselves into a highly respected caste. There were hardly any conversions outside of it, and they did not show much interest in converting others to Christ until very recently.

Francis Xavier (1506–1552) was the first Catholic missionary to go to India. Motivated by a desire to protect the Roman Church against attack by the Protestant Reformers, many young men and women devoted their lives to the preaching of the gospel in lands beyond Europe. Xavier adopted several controversial methods for conversion, including forced conversion of the natives in the Portuguese colonies in India and forced interracial marriages of Indian women with Portuguese soldiers. His major focus was on the conversion of fishermen all over the coastal regions of India. There is at present a substantial number of Catholic fishermen from the Indian peninsula.

Bartholomew Ziegenbalg (1683–1719) was the first Protestant missionary from Europe to go to India. He was chosen and sent by the King of Denmark and Norway to evangelize the Danish colony of a small port town in Tamil country, Tranquebar. A German by birth, Ziegenbalg was a student at Halle when August Francke, the leader of the Pietist movement, recommended him to the king. He died very young (in his late thirties), but within a short span of about fifteen years, Ziegenbalg established a pattern for future Christian missions in India.

Ziegenbalg learned the Tamil language in eighteen months, established a church for natives, rescued the children of mixed marriages (between the natives and the European soldiers and businessmen) from Roman Catholic baptism, brought them under Lutheran baptism, established and ran public schools, translated the Bible into Tamil, and wrote catechisms for the natives. He suffered much torture, both physical and mental, at the hands of the Danish governor, who was not interested in evangelization.

Ziegenbalg studied Hinduism and wrote an insightful description and analysis of its theology and rituals. He was severely reprimanded for his study, because the mission board at that time felt that he was sent to evangelize the Indians, not to record their faith. His story is a great inspiration to all who would like to go overseas to do what God wants them to do in obedience to His call.

There are many missionaries who devoted their lives to the evangelization of Hindus. William Carey, the father of modern Protestant missions, who labored among the Bengali Hindus and Muslims, is perhaps the most well known among all these missionaries. Amy Carmichael and Pandita Rama Bai are two great women missionaries who served the Lord faithfully among the poor and needy in India. Stanley Jones, Sadhu Sundersingh, C. F. Andrews, J. C. Arulappan, Vaman Tilak, Lesslie Newbigin, Stephen Neil—the list is endless.

The caste hierarchy and divisions among Hindus continue to pose great problems for the church. Roman Catholic missionaries allowed caste divisions within their church, as did Protestants in the past. When they realized that caste divisions and passions act against basic Christian charity, they tried to make amends, but caste had already taken deep roots. When the converts were urged to give up their castes and accept all Christians as sons of Christ, the upper-caste Christians left the church in large numbers. Even now, there is strong resistance to Christ at the top of caste hierarchy. This leads to the stigma among Hindus that Christianity is the religion of the lower castes, and this imposed stigma further hinders the receptivity to the gospel among members of the upper castes.

Just as Hindus are given to devotion to their gods, in preaching the gospel we need to emphasize devotion to Jesus. Devotion and related behavioral disciplines come easily to Hindus; a Hindu always seeks to meet his personal needs. We need to emphasize the fact that

Christ is a personal, living God who is always merciful and who takes care of His creation.

Hindus are impressed by the healing powers of Jesus Christ. We can narrate the incidences of healing by Jesus found in the Bible, and explain that He heals not only the physical condition but also brings us closer to himself. Hindus tend to understand the importance and relevance of spiritual matters in the context of day-to-day living.

Because of the divergence in the religious modes of Brahmans and non-Brahmans, a message of personal freedom and mental peace is applicable. While witnessing to a Brahman or an upper-caste Hindu, emphasize salvation, intellectually definable duties, and good morals. Speak about the authority of Jesus as Lord and Savior. Compare certain religious concepts such as those found in the Rig-veda or the Upanishads that focus on one Universal, personal Being and propitiation for sins. These persons are able to relate to these ideas and are likely to engage you in further conversation.

When witnessing to a Hindu belonging to a lower caste or to uneducated people, talk more about the social justice and personal comfort and joy Jesus offers. Speak of His help in times of special need, and how He grants our heart's desires if we obey His Word. These words will strike a sympathetic chord in the hearts of these men and women.

Do not put the story of Jesus Christ in historical terms, placing Him in the midst of Israel. Rather, focus on Jesus as God, who revealed himself to all humankind and who promises to lead all people to total liberation from superstition, poverty, and fear. Tell the simple story of Jesus, emphasizing His saving grace for all peoples. Although Jesus was a real person in history, it is not necessary to define His geographical limitation when He was on earth.

To start with, it is best to avoid stories from the Old Testament. Also avoid talking about membership in a church, or even baptism, in the beginning stages of your contact. Emphasis must be on personal devotion to Jesus in contrast to the continuation of vestiges of idolatry and pantheism.

Give your Hindu brother freedom of choice—no coercion, and no pressure, for these will create fear in him about estrangement from his kin. If, in a family, you know that one partner knows Christ, encourage the Christian to hold to his or her faith with patience against all odds. The Christian partner could read the Bible and talk about the principles and stories in it to his or her Hindu relatives. The Christian has the opportunity and privilege to live a life of Christian love and faith so that his or her family may come to recognize that these are distinctive qualities of Christianity. There are thousands of interreligious marriages taking place among Hindus, many partners of which will ultimately be drawn to Christ, as was the author of this book.

Finally, do not enter into argument about the folly of Hindu gods. Simply narrate the story of Jesus and quote what He said. Remember that saving souls for Christ is our goal, not establishing the superiority of the Christian religion.

FOLK RELIGIOUS HINDUS

4

Almost without exception, every Hindu follows some folk religious tradition. These folk practices may or may not have any sanction in the Hindu sacred scriptures, but the detail in literature is amazing. For example, Hindu almanacs, sold in countless millions, often list the predicted consequences a person would face in daily life if a lizard fell on him. These are so tabulated that the consequence one faces when a lizard falls on his head is different from the ones he may face if it falls on his chest.

If a person has plans to travel east to reach his destination, he first consults the almanac: is it wise for him to travel east on that day? One day of the week may be good for travel west, while another may be better for travel east, etc. Even a single day may be split into several favorable and unfavorable periods. Hindus are expected to begin their ventures only when the day and the period within the day are auspicious. Anything started unfavorably is bound to fail and bring suffering and loss to the person and his family. Such notions govern every walk of life.

When a Hindu who follows the traditional beliefs steps out of his house, he looks for omens. If a cat crosses his path, he stops and returns home or rests for a while before resuming his trip. He sees good and bad signs all around him. He looks to the flight of the birds and determines future happenings. He thinks that the movement of the celestial bodies in the zodiac rules his life; he seeks to know his future material prospects, health, and longevity by reading them. He believes that by propitiating the smaller deities through animal sacrifices and through various food offerings, he may be able to get what he wants.

Social traditions and folk religious traditions often merge together in the mind of a folk Hindu. A person born into a family that practices folk Hinduism more than the scriptural religion often becomes somewhat cynical and gives up many folk religious beliefs when he goes to school and receives formal education. Even so, he is never able to shake off all these beliefs because he and his community (or caste) have been following them for generations. Moreover, he also sees that the people of other castes who practice the Hindu scriptural religion, such as those belonging to the Brahman communities, still practice similar folk beliefs. The Brahman priest does not generally interfere with anyone's tradition, as such; each caste is entitled to have its own religious beliefs within the Hindu fold.

As I mentioned earlier, millions of Hindus experience only folk religion. While they see that their religion may consist of more than what they know, and even when they may feel that what they practice may not be appropriate within the scriptural Hindu religion, still it is acceptable, for it is the only kind of religion their families have known for generations.

FOLK RELIGION BREEDS FEAR

The folk religious Hindu is motivated by fear, believing that any suffering or loss is due to his failure to make sufficient sacrifices and offerings to his deity. Stated another way, for every good thing he needs from the spiritual powers, he is required to make an offering of some sort, and so his approach is based on fear.

An educated Hindu coming from a folk religious family (especially one belonging to a caste other than the Brahman community) is generally not sure of the foundations of his religion. He recognizes the general trends of Hindu thought but is not truly connected to them. He is certainly more at home with Hinduism than with the teachings and practices of other religions, such as Christianity, but at the same time his heart often is not in it.

It is the folk Hindu who is better prepared to see the sacrifice that Jesus made for all humanity. He knows that this world is full of spirits, because of the sacrifices and offerings made in his folk religion. He also sees more easily the injustice that surrounds this world in every walk of life; it is likely that he has had to overcome many forms of unfairness. He may be from an agriculturist family or a household of landless laborers. He may be the first person or one among the few in his family, area, village, or town, or even his caste, to go to college and experience the benefits of modern education. It is possible that his own siblings did not have the opportunity he had, either because of their lack of motivation or because of limited family resources. Thus a conversation about the social background of the person you meet is bound to throw light on his folk religious beliefs. He is likely to conceal the fact that he believes in or follows folk religious practices, because most Indians believe that openly admitting to it is superstitious and is not the sign of an educated person.

CHARACTERISTICS OF FOLK HINDUISM

Since folk religion is pervasive among Hindus, it is important for us to understand its obvious characteristics. A folk religious Hindu often believes in the existence and operation of the spirits, recognizing that there may be good as well as evil spirits, noble and ignoble. Some spirits may be caring and others indifferent, and still others outright harmful. However, the gods he worships may not be equated with the spirits; the gods have a separate level of existence and functions to perform. The spirits of dead people, especially those who met with an untimely death, need to be propitiated at regular intervals so that they may rest in peace and not cause any harm to their families. While an educated folk Hindu may not believe much regarding the spiritual realm, he performs rituals because this is what is done in his family and because he has a certain fear about the spirits.

Folk Hindus "maneuver" the spirits by making suitable offerings, by conjuring with magical words, by offering blood sacrifices, or even by threatening them with the help of more powerful spirits. They perform ceremonies and carefully avoid tabooed objects or persons. They obtain charms and talismans to tap and store the power of the spirits.

A folk Hindu believes in the inherent power of certain objects, persons, and places, and the power of the objects or persons is revealed through the result of the ritual. If there is no immediate result beneficial to them, folk Hindus are willing to transfer their attachment from one object or person to another. Often they have such immense faith in and dependence on these elements that they are willing to wait for long periods to get the result they desire. The inherent power is called by several names, and this power is neutral in the sense that it can be tapped by or inherent in any person, moral or immoral.

Another characteristic is that a folk Hindu believes in the close relationship between man, animals, and nature. Hindus worship not only idols of gods but also living things such as cows, bulls, plants, trees, birds, and snakes. (Serpent worship is widely prevalent among folk Hindus.)

Belief in the power of special words is common throughout the spectrum of Hinduism. Some people hold on to the syllables given to them by their gurus and recite them, usually silently. Others recite the names of their gods aloud or silently or even write them a number of times every day. Still others recite verses from the sacred scriptures. While these are personal practices of the Hindu devotee, there is immense faith in the power of the spoken word.

Through the incantation of magical words, the powers inherent in the objects are tapped. Sometimes the words are inscribed on talismans and charms, and people wear them to ward off evil spirits. These words have the function of petitioning the spirits or gods and are not prayers in the Christian sense.

For thousands of years, Hindus have believed that by proper and perfect pronunciation of words addressed to their gods, they would be able to please and influence them and release power for their benefit. Wrong pronunciation could result in bad effects; prayers should be repeated often and perfectly for better results. The prayers are often in a fixed form with fixed words, the meaning of which may or may not be known to the person who recites them. Since the folk Hindu does not understand Sanskrit scripture, he simply follows the particular practices handed down in his family and caste.

When animals are offered as sacrifice, they are normally killed in a ceremonious manner (with a single stroke), and the blood is drained—the blood being the essence of the victim. But even with sacrifices things can go wrong, and the gods and spirits may not respond favorably. When this happens, the sacrificer blames himself, his fate, and his stars, or he blames the procedures he adopted for the failure, but never the spirits or gods. It may be that the spirits were under coercion from some other more powerful spirits, but the participation of the gods and spirits is not questioned. However, there is also the possibility that after repeated ceremonies that do not bring about the desired results, the worshipers may decide that the spirits and gods have lost their original powers, and they move on to supplicate newly emerging ones.

Hindus in general observe many ceremonies—to prevent personal calamities, to receive new benefits, or simply to commemorate the activities of the spirits and gods in the past; or they may be done in conjunction with the rites of passage of the worshipers and their family members. Folk religious Hindus are greatly influenced by various taboos; the objects from which power emanates or that represent power should be handled with great care. Often these are not to be touched or even their names said aloud. Likewise, if they want to please the spirits, they should not see, touch, or eat unclean objects lest the sacred power be lost. While others may see this as a bondage that individuals have to put up with, folk religious Hindus think of this as tradition, and following traditions brings merit before the gods and spirits; yet even if no merit accrues, they are free from the danger that may be caused if the taboo is broken. Tradition and taboo go hand in hand; sometimes they become identical, and only the taboo remains as the tradition.

Folk religious Hindus often use fetishes, valuing them because they think the spirits and gods operate through them—that they are storehouses of the powers of the spirits. Charms and talismans are available for sale, and the folk Hindu is eager to buy and wear them to ward off evil powers or to tap the powers in his favor. If a person known to possess spirit power has prayed over and personally prepared these objects, it is believed they may have even more powers.

It is difficult to distinguish clearly between charms and fetishes. Charms or amulets are objects that have magical powers to bring their wearer good fortune or protect him from harm—pieces such as thin copper metallic sheets on which some verses or mantra are written. A fetish is usually an object of nature in which a spirit dwells: claws, teeth, horns, bones, or other parts of animals; shells, stones, leaves, pieces of wood or metal, rags, or even refuse.

Visiting a teacher or guru, and paying obeisance to him or her, is quite common for all classes of Hindus, and gurus have become essential symbols of the rejuvenated classical Hinduism of the intellectuals. However, this practice of going to other humans and seeking their help for predicting the future, ameliorating the present malady, and, if necessary, causing harm to the enemy of the worshiper, was widely prevalent among folk religious Hindus long before the modern reemergence of the gurus.

Village priests and shamans are known to be the mediators of spirits, having direct contact with them. The gods and spirits visit them and possess them, putting them into a trance and giving them the ability to find out why the spirits are angry or why they are coming to help. They foretell both future calamities and successes that await the worshiper, and they also indicate what steps of placation are needed to satisfy them.

Shamans may or may not be the priests in the village temples. They usually work for a fee among members of a community to meet individual spiritual needs. The fee is not highlighted, but the first step in tapping the power of the shaman is to make an offering to the gods—in reality, an offering to the shaman. Shamans often are sought to do harm to the enemies of their client or to remove the harm done to them by the enemy. They supposedly have magic words, charms, fetishes, and divination powers.

Shamans operate in secrecy; however, they are not all "spirit-led" and may also accomplish what they want by sleight of hand. Shamanism is, indeed, a booming phenomenon all over India—from the rural areas the practice has spread into the cities in great strength. Highly educated individuals may refrain from going to the village shaman, but they are still given to telepathy and other modern practices of spiritism. An interesting fact about Hindu folk religion is that while educated individuals and those brought up in the tradition of intellectual Hinduism may despise it and look down upon it, folk Hinduism is transformed into modern spiritism in the practices of intellectual Hindus.

Magic, ordeal, and divination are commonly used among folk Hindus who think their suffering may be due to black magic performed against them by their enemies. To ward off evil, they often hire shamans and priests to perform special worship procedures in secrecy. They organize these periodically so that any evil that may have been released against them can be checked.

Ordeals may be used to determine the status of people charged with crimes; for instance, the suspect may be asked to dip his hands in boiling hot water or oil to prove his innocence. While such instances are on the wane, the practice is not entirely abolished.

A devout Hindu may subject himself to ordeals as a form of penance. Sometimes he pierces his tongue or his back with needles. He may roll himself all the way to the temple. He may walk over burning coals or carry a pot of burning coals on his head.

Witchcraft and sorcery are also quite common among folk Hindus, a flourishing business in villages, small towns, and even in modern cities. Medicine is another area where folk Hinduism plays a crucial role: people believe that the cure obtained through modern medicine is either incomplete or temporary, and full cure or recovery is possible only if the spirits are consulted and cajoled. Often folk Hindus classify illnesses in terms of those that can be cured by medicine and those that can be cured only by ensuring the participation of the spirits through shamans.

While Hindus of all classes adopt some form of ancestor worship or veneration, folk Hindus remember the dead as if they were living persons through offerings of clothes or objects for personal hygiene such as combs, mirrors, soaps, etc. Folk Hindus are afraid of the dead in their families, and if the dead person was bad before he died, extra care supposedly must be taken to appease him after his death.

Folk Hindus look at religion as family, and caste tradition as a means to draw power from the spiritual realm. They may notice that the priests, shamans, and gurus they go to for help and counseling are not morally upright, but this does not deter them—they look only for the spirit-power that these people are supposed to have. They sometimes marvel at how people deficient in moral values have power, but they usually discount it as a sign of the strange and mysterious ways of their gods and spirits.

How Do We Reach Folk Hindus With the Gospel?

To reach folk Hindus with the gospel, we must tell them that the fruit of worshiping the true God is "love, joy, peace, patience, kindness, goodness, faithfulness, gentleness and self-control" (Galatians 5:22–23). *They know this intuitively and also through the sayings of the sages in their own religion,* and yet they continue to worship the gods and spirits that lead them astray and only enslave them. These do not enable them to take a strong opposition to a life of "discord, jealousy, fits of rage, selfish ambition, dissensions, factions and envy; drunkenness, orgies, and the like" (Galatians 5:19–21).

Hindus often claim that they recognize the omnipresence of God more than adherents to any other system of faith. However, they do not recognize that they are equating creation with the Creator, and thereby degrade the Lord. To identify God with nature makes God finite and does not regard Him as eternal. Equating God with the material world amounts to denying His personal character.

God came to us in the incarnation of Jesus Christ. It is important to show Hindus how dependence on and worship of material objects does not bring glory to God. Hindus recognize that material objects must be infused with divine power; the question is to what purpose, and what power is being called upon? God himself is available to us for all our needs. He is close at hand if only we will seek Him.

Another curiosity is that a folk religious Hindu worships gods and spirits that have the same weaknesses he does—they quarrel among themselves, plot against one another, take sides with people, and may not hesitate to tell lies and do evil to others. The gods are organized in a way that closely resembles the social hierarchy; what kind of justice, then, can these gods mete out? They themselves are subject to corrupt influence—how can their worshipers expect loyalty from them?

The average Hindu is aware of these facts. However, the fear of the gods and spirits and the age-old traditions compel him to cling to his belief system. Narrating the life history of Jesus and His supreme sacrifice for all of us is a good beginning. We can gently remind the Hindu brother or sister that even as God wants us to follow Him and be truthful in all we do, God himself is quite willing to help us in our difficulties. It is important to tell and to demonstrate how we do not try to offer something material to God in order to obtain His help. We pray and trust that He is listening and answering our prayers according to His will; once we surrender ourselves to the will of God, we leave everything to Him and accept the result as His plan.

Of course, it is also important to emphasize that such surrender does not mean that we then do nothing to further our cause. We do everything in our power, but in keeping with the guidelines of the Word of God. We do not sacrifice, offer material things, or try to overcome evil by using another evil power (Romans 12:21). We believe that God is in control of our lives, and this gives us peace and comfort even as we work to accomplish His will on the earth.

Our faith in God and surrender to His will is not fatalism, as it may appear to a Hindu, nor is it born out of laziness or indifference. Because God has created this world, and since we believe that everything that flows from His hand is good, we love His creation and desire to live our lives for His honor and glory.

So the pleasures of this world are not against God, but seeking *only* the pleasures of this world and putting them above God's creation and over the Creator himself is wrong. Dependence on gods and spirits, on material objects for power and healing, means giving to these things the status of a mediator. The only Mediator between the living God and us is His Son Jesus Christ.

It is important to remember when sharing the truth of the living God with Hindus, or with anyone, to present it with evidence but never in a confrontational manner. There is much in the day-to-day life of a folk religious Hindu that goes against Christian belief and faith, but if we only confront and condemn these practices we risk shutting him off from truly hearing the good news of Christ and possibly becoming His follower. We must gently and lovingly share what Jesus taught us through His Word.

IDENTIFYING FOLK RELIGIOUS HINDUS

How do we know that a person practices folk Hinduism and not classical or elitist Hinduism?

When you encounter a Hindu in your workplace or anywhere else, take the initiative to start a conversation, conducted in an encouraging tone. Often the Hindu is reluctant to speak to a stranger, but if you present yourself as a sympathetic person, not domineering or scornful, he or she may be willing to speak to you on a regular basis. Sometimes what we do naturally, without any intention of judging others, can appear or sound offensive to someone of a minority group. Initiating conversation with a simple greeting and a non-controversial topic is a good beginning.

If you meet a Hindu in a public place, it is never correct to ask about which caste he belongs to. Even in India, this is considered in poor taste. Modern education discourages such questions, unless you are well acquainted with the person and are certain he or she will not take offense. Such a question could be compared to asking another American how much salary he makes in a year.

CONVERSATION STARTERS

(1) *Ask where your Hindu friend comes from.* Is it a large city? A small town? You can ask him to show you where his home is located on a map of India. Most people are interested in talking about their hometown, and also about where they studied, worked, or traveled. This gives a person the opportunity to mentally revisit where he grew up and the environment in which he worked or studied. Usually this is a pleasant experience, bringing with it good memories. Getting to know someone in this way develops empathy.

(2) *Ask what language or languages she speaks.* Where did she learn English or other languages? Does she read materials in her mother tongue? What does she read? Questions of this nature reveal something of a person's background while giving some idea as to whether offering a Christian tract or portion of Scripture would be appropriate. Often people from India prefer to read such literature in English if they are fluent. Some would rather read in their own language. Of course, Christian materials in their language would be an added benefit.

(3) *Ask about his family.* Questions about parents in India will generally bring out the person's social background and reveal some of his religious moorings. If his parents are highly educated and work for the government or a large corporation, for instance, the person may have some independent thinking and attitudes and perhaps be open to discussion about his religion. If he is from an agriculturist family or labor class, he will be more acquainted with folk religious practices.

(4) *Ask about her siblings and what they do.* Often the social and economic status of older siblings will indicate her family background. Asking information about siblings and other family members is normal in conversation among people from India and the Indian subcontinent. Just as in any friendship, it is normal to show interest in the family of the individual.

(5) *Ask particulars about his education.* Did he stay with his parents when he went to college, or in a dormitory? Students moving out of their homes and going away to college have many opportunities to become exposed to new ideas and new ways of life, often very different from what they knew while at home. At present, modern Hindu revivalist movements are very strong among students, who

consequently often begin to hold strong views against other religions, especially Christianity. By God's abundant grace, even in these circumstances, many Hindu students coming from agriculturist and labor classes, whose families practice folk religion, come to take a generous view of the Christian faith.

(6) *Ask who her friends are.* Do they come from the same city, town, or village? Depending on who her friends are and where they come from, your friend may or may not be exposed to new ideas and cultures on an intimate basis.

(7) *Ask what holy days his family celebrates, why, and how.* While there are several holy days celebrated by all Hindus of intellectual, ritual, or folk religious persuasion, there are holy days that are celebrated *only* by folk practitioners. These may vary from family to family, caste to caste, region to region, and ethnic group to ethnic group. When your friend lists the holy days and begins describing them, find out whether his family or caste or ethnic group alone celebrates them, or whether all Hindus do so.

(8) *What holy days does she participate in with her friends?* Does she have any specific personal preference, and why? This conversation will give you an idea whether or not your friend personally observes days honored by her religion or whether she left those traditions behind when she left her family home.

(9) *What does his family do during holy days? Or what did they do, if he has left his family home.* Look for references to the performance of special rituals. Who officiates these rituals? Is a priest specially invited? Does he or the family recite sacred scriptures in Sanskrit? Did they memorize these scriptures early in life? If not, you may be reasonably sure that he comes from a family that practices some form of folk religion. However, it is possible that children from non-Brahman communities may be encouraged to commit to memory Sanskrit verses. In fact, there is a concerted move among the Hindu reformers to encourage children in schools to do the same.

(10) *What is her daily religious routine?* Does it include specific rituals, prayers, or reading? What significance do these rituals have for her in her adult life on her own?

(11) *What is your friend's name and its significance?* Is it the name of an important Hindu god or the name of a folk deity in his area? Trends in naming children do change periodically all over the world; however, naming children after gods is still the most popular practice

among Hindus. Parents have a choice between naming their children after the gods of ritual Hinduism or after smaller village gods; often those who practice folk religion name their children after their family deities.

(12) *Does your friend dress differently when performing rituals?* In other words, does he wear some special attire for the occasion? Ritual Hindus often wear their native garments while performing the rituals, but folk religious Hindu practices do not generally insist on this.

(13) *Does your friend's family or caste have its own family/caste temple?* The temples maintained by specific castes often practice a mix of folk and ritual Hinduism. In rural areas, the temples maintained by the agriculturists and laborers often practice only folk Hinduism. Going on a pilgrimage to ritual Hindu temples is common, and yet on a day-to-day basis, it is the village temple that is more often visited.

(14) *How frequently does your friend visit the temple?* Does he feel deprived if he cannot do so often? Did he visit the temple every day in India or only on special occasions? Was he in the habit of going to the temple when he or his relatives or friends were sick in order to ask for divine favor? Does he think temple worship is an important duty for a Hindu or is it enough to celebrate the holy days and observe the rituals?

(15) *Is the temple that she visited located in the area where her family lived or in a larger city?* Do people from other communities visit this temple? If your friend was in the habit of visiting the ritual Hindu temple, usually located in a place that is frequented by all communities, you can infer that she is aspiring to become a Hindu of intellectual or ritual persuasion.

(16) *Are daily worship rituals performed in this temple?* What is the caste background of the temple priest? Does he recite Sanskrit verses during worship? During festival days/nights, do the priests and worshipers go into a trance?

(17) *Does her family perform rituals to the dead?* How frequently is this done? Are the rituals performed inside or outside the house?

(18) *Does he believe in the efficacy of the various rituals performed?* This discussion will reveal if the rituals he participates in are done as a matter of tradition and habit or if they have become a significant part of his faith.

Even without directly asking your friend which religious form he follows, you should be able to identify it through some of these questions and conversation. Does he recite Sanskrit verses on a regular basis when he performs his religious ceremonies? Does he have pictures or images of gods that are not commonly worshiped by those following elitist Hindu religion? Does he belong to a family that offers animal sacrifices? Is his family into the worship of deities that are caste-specific? Is he interested in sectarian quarrels among the Hindus?

Remember, it is not acceptable to ask point blank the caste background of individuals, but again, you will have a good idea by the time you ask a few non-threatening questions. It is impossible to get away from one's caste background even for Christians in India; caste is still an integral part of one's identity and ethos, especially for the person coming from a small town or village.

Simple, friendly conversations should always be emphasized first; giving tracts and Bible portions would come much later. If you rush to give literature, people think you are more interested in giving your religious viewpoint than in getting to know them. The true purpose of evangelism is to first know your neighbor and love him as he is. This means that we respect his feelings and faith even as we pray that he would come to know Jesus as Lord and Savior. Whether or not a person eventually accepts Christ should not be the driving force in our meeting a Hindu neighbor—showing our love and acceptance is the most important first step. When the Lord opens their hearts, there will be an urge to know His Word if we have faithfully represented Him to them. Until then, we should not impose our personal theology.

Of course, showing respect and consideration for our neighbor does not mean that we never share our faith. Even Hindus do not mind our praying to Jesus for their welfare. And nothing should deter us from telling the stories and parables of Jesus when an occasion presents itself. Citing the Proverbs, sharing incidents in the ministry of Jesus, telling how God cares for those who put their trust in Him, and explaining the significance of your faith and behavior through concrete illustrations go a long way in awakening the curiosity and the spirit of a Hindu friend.

DEVELOP A RECIPROCAL RELATIONSHIP

When you initiate a friendship with a Hindu neighbor, it is natural that he will have questions about you. Some of these may sound awkward or overly personal because in North American culture certain questions are not raised on a casual basis—such as why you are still single and not married, why you do not have children, or what your salary is. Don't think that your Hindu neighbor is too inquisitive or is stepping over the line by asking such questions. You can either answer him or tell him that in your culture these questions are not usually asked.

You should recognize that in a dialogue both parties have equal rights to ask questions and to answer or not as he or she sees fit. There are bound to be some awkward moments when two cultures meet. Your Hindu friend may expect openness from you, and if he does, use it as an opportunity to show friendliness and gentleness. Acts of kindness can be expressed in many ways: Look for opportunities to reveal that you are concerned about his needs and welfare. Genuine caring speaks for itself and becomes the strongest bridge between persons. Of course, no amount of human effort will ever make our love constantly genuine. Only God can make our love have this quality. Remember Paul's words about love: It covers a multitude of sins. And it always hopes, always perseveres.

If you maintain regular contact and conversation with your Hindu friend, there will always be opportunities to speak about spiritual matters. Assuming he knows that you are a Christian, and having realized that you as a Christian are not imposing on him your theology, he may be more open to start talking about his own beliefs, or he may have certain needs that he would like you to pray for. Just as in any friendship, it is not advisable that every conversation you have should revolve around religious or spiritual matters. Maintain a healthy balance.

When the occasion arises, do not hesitate to state what you believe and why. Your Hindu friend who comes from a folk religious background will have questions about the Christian faith. We never know where the conversation will go or how the Holy Spirit will move. Submit yourself to His working. Do not plan to always finish what you started in your conversation; plan rather to be sensitive to the voice of the Spirit and to your friend's feelings.

BASIC CHRISTIAN TRUTHS

5

Some of the essential Christian truths that should be shared with Hindu neighbors are as follows:

THE IMMANENCE AND TRANSCENDENCE OF GOD

God is immanent (near) as well as transcendent (far); He lives in our heart, and we are His temple. Therefore, it is important to keep our body, soul, and spirit pure by the power of His Spirit. God is *present* everywhere, but He is not part of all creatures, as pantheism states.

The Bible informs us in Acts 17:28 that "in Him we live and move and have our being." In Colossians 1:16–17, we learn that "by Him all things were created: things in heaven and on earth, visible and invisible, whether thrones or powers or rulers or authorities; all things were created by him and for him." A major difference between God and His creatures is that God is infinite, while His creatures are finite.

We must recognize that God is unique, different from everything else in creation. We are made in the image of God, but we are not the same essence as God—we do not emanate from God's nature. It is also important to understand that the ultimate goal of salvation is not merging with or absorption into God, as Hindus believe, but a continued fellowship with God.

Hindus generally think that becoming one with God is their

ultimate salvation, calling this super-spirituality. According to the Bible, this is not acceptable. It is an idolatrous position to put God and creation as one. We are to abide in Him in the sense of fellowship, but we don't become one with Him in the sense of being equal. Christians respect and love nature as the creation of God, but we do not worship it as a god or spirit. We may respect people who are considered to be great by people of other religions, but we do not bow down before them or worship them. A guru or spiritual leader cannot be considered a manifestation of divine power in human form; worship of *any* individual or object is forbidden. John 8:23 tells us that Jesus is from above and we are from below—we are of this world and He is not.

Christians also hold that while God is separate from creation, He is active throughout the world and throughout history in the lives of humankind and all He has made; He is the Sustainer, Guide, and Governor of the universe. Psalm 104 declares how God is involved in our lives and in everything that surrounds us: "How many are your works, O LORD!" and "these all look to you to give them their food at the proper time" (104:24, 27).

The Bible says that God is always at hand, immanent in us if we repent of our sins and confess Him as our Lord and Savior:

> For this is what the high and lofty One says—he who lives forever, whose name is holy: "I live in a high and holy place, but also with him who is contrite and lowly in spirit, to revive the spirit of the lowly and to revive the heart of the contrite" (Isaiah 57:15).

> "I will walk among you and be your God, and you will be my people" (Leviticus 26:12).

GOD IS PERSONAL

God's Word says that He is a Person, a personal Being who reveals himself by His names, such as Yahweh (Exodus 3:13–15; Isaiah 42:8); He knows and wills (1 Corinthians 2:10–11; Ephesians 1:11). He *is* the Creator and Preserver of all nature, but He is not simply worshiped for this reason; while many religions look to the Supreme Being mostly as an original Designer of nature and stand in awe of Him, the Bible says that God is an *active* participant in history, controlling and directing the affairs of all humanity and entering into a personal relationship with us. God does not look at His creation as an object of *leela* (sport); He does not distance himself from what He has made and leave it to its own "fate." Through His participation in and guidance of history, He is at hand to help, having entered into covenant with humanity.

This covenant character of God shows His personhood. Moreover, He is described as Father: Jesus referred to Him as "my Father," "your Father," and "the heavenly Father." The fatherhood of God reveals His eternal care for the creation, even as He is the Source and Sustainer of it. God is our Father (Matthew 5:45; 6:26–32), and we can always put our trust in Him for our well-being.

God is a Person, not an abstract First Cause or Vital Force. He is all love, but to say that love is God is not a correct characterization. Hindus say this, but God is not an abstract quality or quantity— again, He is a personal Being. He is always at hand for those who put their trust in Him and seek Him fervently.

Love is not God; love is an inherent *attribute* of God. Hindus, in contrast, elevate attributes or qualities to the *status* of God. One primary reason for this is that the gods created by Hindus are fashioned out of the attributes they wish to make prominent.

GOD IS SPIRIT

God is neither man nor force nor object; we cannot reduce the personhood of God to any of these. God is Spirit, and we must worship Him in spirit and in truth (John 4:24). This necessarily stops us from portraying Him in images and worshiping them as God. The spiritual nature of God reveals His infinite nature; creation is flesh, but God is Spirit.

As Spirit, God is the living God, the fountain of life (Psalm 36:9). God has life in himself (John 5:26); on the other hand, men and matter are *given* spirit, while God *is* pure Spirit, the Source of all other life: "The breath of the Almighty gives me life" (Job 33:4); "When you send your Spirit, they are created, and you renew the face of the earth" (Psalm 104:30).

Since God is Spirit, we cannot derive Him from any material thing. As we have already pointed out, this is one of the primary reasons why children of God should never worship images and why such worship is prohibited (Exodus 20:4; Deuteronomy 4:12, 15–18).

Because God is Spirit, He can be worshiped anywhere; He cannot be contained in any particular place or space.

GOD IS HOLY

God is "the Holy One," incomparable: " 'To whom will you compare me? Or who is my equal?' says the Holy One" (Isaiah 40:25); "The LORD our God is holy" (Psalm 99:9).

The holiness of God indicates His divine separateness and sacredness; wonder, awe, and fear are felt in the hearts of those who contemplate Him. The Hebrew word for "holy" refers to the state of being separate from sin, and moral perfection distinguishes God from all creation. For followers of God to be acceptable to Him, we must be holy—separate and distinct from the sins that permeate this world. While gods in Hinduism are considered to be divine, there is an important contrast between them and the living God.

Everyone will agree that many Hindu gods do not measure up to moral perfection; Hindus will seek to explain away their flawed behavior and motives. But "God is not a man, that he should lie, nor a son of man, that he should change his mind. Does he speak and then not act? Does he promise and not fulfill?" (Numbers 23:19). You need to emphasize the need for a truthful conception of God that is morally and ethically perfect, even by human reason. If gods that are assumed to have powers superior to humans are immoral and unethical, how could humans be expected to be moral and ethical?

GOD IS PERFECT

God is without blemish; we read in Deuteronomy 32:4 that "He is the Rock, his works are perfect, and all his ways are just. A faithful God who does no wrong, upright and just is he." In the Sermon on the Mount, Jesus commands that we be perfect as our heavenly Father is perfect. God is light, and there is no darkness in Him at all (1 John 1:5).

GOD IS OUR FATHER

God is our Father, not only in the spiritual sense of being our Creator but also in the active sense of sustaining all creation. His care for people is one of fatherly love and concern: The Bible says that we are the "children of the LORD [our] God" (Deuteronomy 14:1). We need to respond to God, then, as children respond to their father; His fatherly love requires us to be obedient to Him:

> How gladly would I treat you like sons and give you a desirable land, the most beautiful inheritance of any nation. I thought you would call me "Father" and not turn away from following me. (Jeremiah 3:19)
>
> "A son honors his father, and a servant his master. If I am a father, where is the honor due me? If I am a master, where is the respect due me?" says the LORD Almighty. (Malachi 1:6)

The ministry of Jesus reveals to us the fatherhood of God—there are more references in the Gospels to God as Father than in any of the other books of the Bible. Jesus refers to His relationship to His Father in a special way, making it clear that He is the Son, equal with the Father, who fulfilled God's purpose regarding the salvation of man and functions as the sole Mediator between God and humanity (Matthew 11:27; John 5:22; 8:58; 10:30, 38; 14:9; 16:28).

CHAPTER

MATERIAL OBJECTS WITH DIVINE POWER?

6

Because Hindus believe in the immanence of gods and spirits, they are given to the worship of material objects, believing God or gods are present within. However, material objects are not God, nor do they contain divine power worthy of our worship. We cannot deny the fact that God's power may be transmitted and demonstrated through objects, persons, and events; since God is Spirit, He can transcend all barriers to express and reveal himself to us. However, treating an object, person, event, or process as a storehouse of power in itself is negating or cheapening the glory of God, and to believe that such power is available at will is to believe a lie.

There is a biblically recorded episode of *total faith* in which a woman who had been subject to bleeding for twelve years was instantaneously healed when she touched the edge of Jesus' cloak:

> As Jesus was on his way, the crowds almost crushed him. And a woman was there who had been subject to bleeding for twelve years, but no one could heal her. She came up behind him and touched the edge of his cloak, and immediately her bleeding stopped. "Who touched me?" Jesus asked. When they all denied it, Peter said, "Master, the people are crowding and pressing against you." But Jesus said, "Someone touched me; I know that power has gone out from me." Then the woman, seeing that she could not go unnoticed, came trembling and fell at his feet. In the presence of all the people, she told why she had touched him and how she had been instantly

healed. Then he said to her, "Daughter, your faith has healed you. Go in peace" (Luke 8:42–48).

She had seen and heard how Jesus healed people: His mere touch gave sight to the blind; the words He spoke drove out evil spirits; the lame started walking at His compassionate encouragement. This woman was desperate and helpless, and her only hope seemed to be in Jesus. He was not demanding sacrifice, fee, or propitiation—His healing was free to all, so she took a stealthy step of faith. An unannounced and undeclared intense trust in His power emboldened her to touch the hem of His garment, and by this act of belief, she declared that Jesus is not a crafty shaman or priest. Her *faith* healed her; so said Jesus.

Note that this incident is not a how-to model for the church in terms of physical contact. We are not mini-Jesuses. People all over the world seek miracles in their favor, and when they find a person performing signs and wonders, they tend to treat him as God and try to get hold of the objects he touched, used, or wore so that they can tap some of his power for their benefit. This has happened even among Christians; however, the Bible clearly denounces such efforts. Look at Acts 14:8–18, where people in Lystra, after witnessing the miraculous healing of the crippled man, began to call Barnabas "Zeus" and Paul "Hermes." They called the people "to turn from these worthless things to the living God." Likewise, in Acts 28:1–6, when Paul "shook the snake off into the fire and suffered no ill effects," the people of Malta "said he was a god," though he was not. God is *Spirit*, transcending everything He has made. To try to contain Him in material objects (even people) is to cheapen His glory. Consider the following story:

> The apostles performed many miraculous signs and wonders among the people. And all the believers used to meet together in Solomon's Colonnade. No one else dared join them, even though they were highly regarded by the people. Nevertheless, more and more men and women believed in the Lord and were added to their number. As a result, people brought the sick into the streets and laid them on beds and mats so that at least Peter's shadow might fall on some of them as he passed by. Crowds gathered also from the towns around Jerusalem, bringing their sick and those tormented by evil spirits, and all of them were healed. (Acts 5:12–16)

To catch the shadow of Peter for healing purposes is to seek the power of God apart from His glory, which certainly is animistic behavior. The focus here is more on the growing popularity of Peter and the apostles than on the power of a shadow—*there is no statement that says that people were healed by Peter's shadow*. This is a description of the animistic beliefs prevailing at that time among the Jews, not an example for us to emulate. Also remember what Peter said to the lame man earlier:

> Silver or gold I do not have, but what I have I give you. In the name of Jesus Christ of Nazareth, walk. (Acts 3:6)
> By faith in the name of Jesus, this man whom you see and know was made strong. It is Jesus' name and the faith that comes through him that has given this complete healing to him, as you can all see. (Acts 3:16)

There is also an amazing set of circumstances reported in the ministry of the apostle Paul. The Word of God calls them "extraordinary" for a special reason: The carrier through which the miracle was performed could be mistaken as the source of power; the focus of attention could turn to the material object rather than to the God who wrought the miracle. To caution against such a tendency, the Word of God calls it extraordinary, "something above the common road of miracles," to use the words of Matthew Henry. Again, the major purpose in using the adjective "extraordinary," it appears to me, is to caution that normally this kind of miracle and consequent behavior is not commonplace or acceptable.

> God did extraordinary miracles through Paul, so that even handkerchiefs and aprons that had touched him were taken to the sick, and their illnesses were cured and the evil spirits left them. (Acts 19:11–12)

This is merely a description of what happened in the ministry of the apostle Paul, who never exalted himself above or placed himself on the same level with Jesus. He delighted in being a truthful and faithful servant, magnifying the name of God, never taking any credit for what was being worked through him by the Spirit. There is no approval of the people's actions, nor is there any exhortation to them to continue in that manner; instead, they were continually encour-

accession of various sorts (and not always legally or uprightly), were ambivalent about the place of Christianity in India almost from the beginning of their rule. Preaching of the gospel was to be a private religious effort, not to be supported by the Crown. There were many incidents in which British officialdom took steps to curb missionary activities. So then, people came to Christ mainly through the voluntary work of the missionaries, not by any support of the ruling British monarchy.

There is no denying that the message of Christ is foreign to Hindu theology. Again, there are so many differences between the two that Hindus, instead of considering it simply foreign to their religion, look at it as a religion of foreigners. To me, theologically speaking, belief in Christ and belief in Hinduism are in conflict with one another (there *are* vast differences between the two), but Christianity is *not* a religion of foreigners: People of different nations, colors, and communities all over the world have embraced Jesus as their Lord and Savior, while remaining as nationalistic and patriotic as ever. In fact, the Word of God ordains submission to governmental authority, and Christians willingly follow the righteous laws of the lands in which they live.

Hindus are willing to embrace "foreign" technologies, become trained in "foreign" warfare, adopt "foreign" eating habits and other ways of life, and cross seas to accumulate wealth, without considering any of these things forbidden or illegal. But when it comes to religion, they consider anything other than Hinduism foreign, even though the church in India is at least a thousand years old, and about thirty million people in India profess to follow Christ.

There is a strange love/hate relationship between the secular social reformers who seek to modernize Hindu communities by doing away with traditions and those who believe in upholding tradition at any cost. Social reformers wish to replace religious practices with secular practices; at the same time, they also encourage a revival of interest in folk culture, religion, and the arts as a part of seeking, establishing, and fostering national, ethnic, and communal identities.

Tradition Defined

Tradition is transmitting established beliefs, customs, ways, or methods from one generation to the next. Tradition is a strong source

aged to depend only on the name of Jesus and to put all their trust in Him for their needs.

The purpose of the miracles was to impress upon people the glory and power of God and to encourage them to become disciples of Jesus Christ. When the name of Jesus was magnified by the miracles wrought in his name, the Bible tells us:

> Many of those who believed now came and openly con-
> fessed their evil deeds. A number who had practiced sorcery
> brought their scrolls together and burned them publicly.
> When they calculated the value of the scrolls, the total came
> to fifty thousand drachmas. In this way the word of the Lord
> spread widely and grew in power. (Acts 19:18–20)

On the other hand, when materials seem to have power in the experience of folk Hindus, the focus is more on the materials them-selves. Instead of leading people to confess their sins, dependence on such objects furthers the selfishness of the individuals and groups that depend on them as storehouses of power.

Why shouldn't we depend on spirits and materials as sources of power and healing? The Bible compares and evaluates spirits in rela-tion to the Holy Spirit (Galatians 5:19–23). Another important rea-son, according to the Word of God, is that dependence on material objects for power and healing means that we give to these things the status of mediator. *The only true mediator is Jesus Christ*: "For there is one God and one mediator between God and men, the man Christ Jesus" (1 Timothy 2:5).

When a folk religious Hindu seeks miracles or remedy from mere objects, he is looking for divine power—the thing itself comes to function as a god for him. Since god can be found in everything, worship of anything is condoned. This is to exchange God for an image—to worship and serve created things rather than the Creator (Romans 1:25).

To summarize, man wants to appropriate power for his benefit, and he seeks this from material objects. When his craze for power is satisfied, he elevates objects to the level of mini-gods by his venera-tion of them. In doing so, he is afraid that if he does not show appro-priate respect, he may lose the power these objects supposedly bestow upon him. This is selfishness rather than the loving worship God asks of us. God's plan for us is to love Him: He turns our fear into love, and the relationship we develop with Him changes from our previous idolatrous slavery into a glorious companionship.

DIVINATION AND
DRAWING LOTS

7

Divination, widely practiced by Hindus of all walks, is born out of a desire to know the significance of the present and to link it with the past and the future. Hindu mythology abounds in stories that use divination, which is also used to know what goes on at present in another place. Hindus do not use the Western phrase "consultation with a psychic."

Diviners are on hand everywhere in India. These may be astrologers, numerologists, naturists, face readers, palm readers, or simply ordinary men and women who are known to have special powers. Hindus by the thousands flock to these people (sometimes traveling hundreds of miles) to seek revelation about the future or remedies for their present suffering. Successful diviners often rent hotel rooms and set up shop; their schedule of arrival and departure in specific places is advertised in popular newspapers. Unsuccessful predictions are many, but those given to seeking the help of diviners easily forget and gloss over such failed oracles and cling to the few successful ones. Many Hindus put an aura of science around certain practices of divination, such as astrology, which is sometimes viewed as based on astronomy. However, there are also many Hindus who do not believe that any branch of divination is scientific.

MEANS OF DIVINATION

Divination often degenerates to the point that anything and everything may be used for its purposes. Dreams, hunches, presentiments, involuntary body actions (such as twitches and sneezes), ordeals, spiritual possession, consulting the dead, observing animal and plant behavior, interpreting the flight of birds or the howling of certain animals, making mechanical manipulations with small objects (such as dice, shells), using playing cards, decoding natural phenomena (such as palmistry or phrenology or astrology), postulating intuitive predictions, and many other forms of divination are employed and followed by Hindus.

The use of animals for divination is quite common. Hindus have an elaborate system of interpreting birdcalls, cries of various animals, lizard movement, and so on. Some of the signs are deadly, while some portend the arrival of guests; some tell in advance of the possibility of sexual union, and some announce an impending death in the family. Parrots may be specially trained to pick a card from the stack in order to divine what is in store for a client. The direction of the flight of eagles is watched and interpreted; sometimes dozens of people, before they start anything of significance on that day, assemble at the riverside and wait there for hours to see in what direction the eagles fly. Others will return to their homes if they see a widow on their way, since this means bad luck. If a donkey brays in the night, it is also a bad omen.

Divination by dreams is also very popular among Hindus, for it is believed that dreams (which everyone may have) communicate the future. That dreams and visions may have something to tell us is not questioned in the Word of God; the message the dreamer brings through his dream is the most important thing, according to the Bible. If the dream or sign or wonder comes true, and the performer or interpreter says, "Let us follow other gods," they will certainly lead to slavery. The Bible clearly indicates that dreams may be deceptive (Zechariah 10:2), and that false prophets often present false dreams in support of their claims. According to the Lord, these people prophesy the delusions of their own minds (Jeremiah 23:25–32).

Divination by ordeal is widespread among folk religious Hindus. A suspect may be asked to dip his or her hand in boiling oil or water or to walk over burning coals. Supposedly, if the person is innocent, he or she will come out unscathed—the divine spirit or Supreme Being will help the innocent to win through the ordeal, while the guilty will be harmed in the process. Another method of divination by ordeal is when the parties swear their innocence before the

Supreme Being, declaring that they will soon die or undergo some other serious consequence if they have uttered lies. Some do die after such a ceremony; however, more often than not, such swearing does not carry much conviction once suspicion against the accused is strong. All this is a manmade process of justice, cruel and inhumane; furthermore, it is coercion, and does not give an opportunity for the accused to prove his innocence.

In 1 Kings (8:31–32) there is a call for justice from God, "condemning the guilty and bringing down on his own head what he has done." However, even here there is no mention of any physical ordeal—it is a request that the innocent be declared innocent and that the guilty be condemned in an appropriate manner. Elsewhere (Exodus 23:6–13) God promises that He will not acquit the guilty and asks us to "have nothing to do with a false charge and do not put an innocent or honest person to death." Invoking other powers and gods leads only to slavery; divination by ordeal is against the Word of God.

TRANCES AND POSSESSION

It is quite common in folk religious Hindu temples and festivals that those who divine fall into an induced trance before they begin the divination process. The spirits that are called upon then possess the individuals. I saw this happen so many times that I often thought this was the only authentic divination; I was not prepared to accept divination by other means, for possession is so dramatic and otherworldly that I was easily convinced of its efficacy. An atmosphere of fear for the person in the trance is created, and whatever he or she blurts out is interpreted as a prophecy of an impending event. Sensory bombardment plays a crucial role.

Summoning the dead is also a common practice used for divination. The deceased, when contacted, allegedly descend on the person who is known to have special power for divination. The voice of the person in the trance then becomes the voice of the dead.

God tells us, "Do not turn to mediums or seek out spiritists, for you will be defiled by them. I am the LORD your God" (Leviticus 19:31).

He also warns us not to imitate the people who indulge in divination:

Do not learn to imitate the detestable ways of the nations there. Let no one be found among you who sacrifices his son or daughter in the fire, who practices divination or sorcery, interprets omens, engages in witchcraft, or casts spells, or who is a medium or spiritist or who consults the dead. Anyone who does these things is detestable to the LORD. . . . You must be blameless before the LORD your God. (Deuteronomy 18:9–13)

When men tell you to consult mediums and spiritists, who whisper and mutter, should not a people inquire of their God? Why consult the dead on behalf of the living? (Isaiah 8:19)

JESUS CAN SET YOU FREE!

If you have been brought up in an atmosphere like the ones just described, you can truly understand and appreciate what it means when the Word of God says that Jesus Christ sets captives free! We need to share this good news with our Hindu neighbors; we need to tell them that putting our trust in Jesus and depending upon Him alone gives us the freedom to ignore such practices and to move forward with the confidence that our Lord is watching over our every step. The Bible says that He is always at hand to help us, and because of Him we are not bound to any evil: Jesus has overcome satanic forces by His crucifixion, death, and resurrection! Any attempt by the Enemy to enslave us will not succeed so long as we place our belief and trust in Jesus and follow Him.

The Bible clearly tells us that we are not to practice divination or sorcery (Leviticus 19:26), which are rebellion (1 Samuel 15:23).

It is for freedom that Christ has set us free. Stand firm, then, and do not let yourselves be burdened again by a yoke of slavery. (Galatians 5:1)

If you hold to my teaching, you are really my disciples. Then you will know the truth, and the truth will set you free. (John 8:31–32)

Now the Lord is the Spirit, and where the Spirit of the Lord is, there is freedom. (2 Corinthians 3:17)

As the occasion arises, share the life of Jesus with your Hindu friends. It is important to tell them the story just as we read it in the Bible; do not garnish it and do not try to compare the life and ministry of Jesus Christ to any noble human individual (or groups of individuals) or the gods of Hinduism. (Such comparison brings in relativism, along with gross misunderstanding.) Tell them how the birth, crucifixion, and resurrection of Jesus were foretold in the Old Testament, using the relevant verses from Isaiah and the other prophets.

For example, in Isaiah 7:14 we read, "Therefore the Lord himself will give you a sign: The virgin will be with child and will give birth to a son, and will call him Immanuel." In Isaiah 11:1–2 we are told, "A shoot will come up from the root of Jesse, from his roots a Branch will bear fruit. The Spirit of the LORD will rest on Him. . . ." Or Micah 5:2: "But you, Bethlehem Ephrathah, though you are small among the clans of Judah, out of you will come for me one who will be ruler over Israel, whose origins are from old, from ancient times." See Isaiah 53 for a vivid description of the life and ministry of Jesus.

In Luke 18:31, Jesus himself refers to what was "written by the prophets about the Son of Man." The New Testament presents Jesus as the fulfillment of the Old Testament messianic prophecies. For instance, in Matthew 1:22–23 we are told, "All this took place to fulfill what the Lord had said through the prophet: 'The virgin will be with child and will give birth to a son, and they will call him Immanuel'—which means, 'God with us.' "

Do not separate the Jesus of faith from the Jesus of history. Often the Hindus, even those of folk religious persuasion, would readily agree on the Jesus of history, taking Him to be a rebel who attacked the rotten social norms of His day. They may also admire His concern for the poor and the needy, and they may even recognize His "special talents" and accept that He was, indeed, performing miracles for the benefit of the people. They may likewise accept that there was some divinity attached to Him in all He did. But when it comes to recognizing him to be God, they will hesitate. Ultimately, many of these people, because of their folk traditions and fear of loss of identity and consequent social shame, may withdraw from taking the final step of acknowledging Jesus as Lord. Since within Hinduism man can become god, it is easy for Hindus to accept Jesus as "a man who became a god." *It is very important that we tell the whole truth.* While it may be necessary to make adjustments in the form and manner of presentation of the story of Jesus, there should be no changing it to suit theological convenience or the comfort of the listener.

That Jesus Christ lived, ministered, and was crucified has been attested in non-Christian as well as Christian sources. However, presenting historical facts as part of sharing our faith with *folk religious Hindus* may not be necessary. Questions relating to the historical Jesus will be raised when we are in dialogue with *elitist* and *intellectual Hindus.*

DRAWING LOTS

Using mechanical means to divine luck and to foretell the future is quite common; the wheel of fortune, for example, is an age-old device. I had an awful habit of tossing a coin to find out whether what I desired would be accomplished, and I would continue to toss it until I got the side of the coin that told me I would get my way. Most cultures at their folk levels have some good luck game or another: The wishbone phenomenon, for example, continues in Western nations, and rolling dice is still practiced for divination purposes.

Drawing lots, perhaps the simplest of all, is a common worldwide practice followed by both elitist and folk religions. In Hindu villages, people go to the local temple and ask the priest to draw lots for them. Often the worshipers themselves draw lots either in front of an idol or in their homes to decide which of the given options they should adopt and to find out if what they desire will be accomplished.

My pastor's wife in India was in the habit of drawing lots to make decisions—to decide on the dates for gospel meetings or to decide on the suitability of the match proposed for a young woman under her care. As a new Christian, I was shocked that believers would do these things. When I asked why she practiced the drawing of lots, she told me that it was biblical: the apostles did it, so why shouldn't we?

[Peter said,] "Therefore it is necessary to choose one of the men who have been with us the whole time the Lord Jesus went in and out among us, beginning from John's baptism to the time when Jesus was taken up from us. For one of these must become a witness with us of his resurrection." So they proposed two men: Joseph called Barsabbas (also known as Justus) and Matthias. Then they prayed, "Lord, you know everyone's heart. Show us which of these two you have chosen to take over this apostolic ministry, which Judas left to go where he belongs." Then they cast lots, and the lot fell to

Matthias; so he was added to the eleven apostles. (Acts 1: 21–26)

WHY WERE LOTS DRAWN?

This was done *before* the Holy Spirit came upon the apostles at Pentecost. Now, with the Holy Spirit as the Comforter and Director of our lives, there is no justification whatsoever for drawing lots to decide on any matter. It is important to pray to the Lord Jesus Christ and to let the Holy Spirit speak to us, giving His direction.

Remember also that the lot is only a mechanical device—the result need not always be true. Haman plotted "to destroy all Mordecai's people, the Jews, throughout the whole kingdom of Xerxes" (Esther 3:6). The lot was cast in Haman's presence to select a day and month for the killing of all Jews, but it turned out that

> when the plot came to the king's attention, he issued written orders that the evil scheme Haman had devised against the Jews should come back onto his own head, and that he and his sons should be hanged on the gallows. (Esther 9:25)

The remembrance of the *Purim* incident described above is, indeed, the declaration of the defeat of drawing lots.

The book of Proverbs declares, "The lot is cast into the lap, but its every decision is from the LORD" (16:33). Casting lots is taken as a tiebreaker, not as a message from God; it is a manmade device to arbitrate disagreements: "Casting the lot settles disputes and keeps strong opponents apart" (Proverbs 18:18).

The hardhearted and unrepentant soldiers, in the act of casting lots for the clothing of Jesus Christ, show that it is not a practice taught by the Holy Spirit.

> They came to a place called Golgotha (which means The Place of the Skull). There they offered Jesus wine to drink, mixed with gall; but after tasting it, he refused to drink it. When they had crucified him, they divided up his clothes by casting lots. (Matthew 27:33–35)

Remember, casting lots is an unreliable medium even for the evil spirits, for often the lot comes to nothing. Dependence on the Holy Spirit's leading brings understanding, wisdom, and a result that is within the will of the Lord.

CHAPTER

ASTROLOGY
8

Astrology comes to us in the guise of a scientific pursuit, the thousands-of-years-old assumption being that the movements of the heavenly bodies have an effect on us—the stars and planets decide the course of our lives, and everything happens according to their position, direction, and movement.

As soon as a child is born, Hindus call an astrologer in order to have a birth horoscope written down. This horoscope charts out the milestones in the infant's life, including how long she will live. Wherever there is a malevolent influence of the planets, the astrologer may suggest propitiatory acts.

On a large scale, Hindus do nothing without reading the horoscope. Choice of spouses, for example, is made based on the match between the horoscopes of the bride and the groom, and some girls may never be able to marry because their horoscopes predict the death of their groom as soon as they are wed. Some predict the death of the father-in-law or mother-in-law, so that the groom's family would be afraid to enter into a marriage relationship with the girl's family; however, there may be some sacrificial arrangements made to overcome the alleged ill effects of the horoscope. Astrology is, in some sense, the worship of the planets; there are also temples for the sun, moon, and stars.

Generally speaking, astrology is considered to be a higher form of religious belief than divination, as it is done using mechanical means (see chapter 7). The astrologer is usually a well-read man, studying the positions and movements of the stars and planets, doing a lot of "mathematical" calculations, drawing charts of the zodiac, and presenting his findings in a language that sounds highly empirical and well-reasoned.

Even people born and brought up in the Christian faith often fall prey to the urge to divine their future. As our civilization becomes more and more individualized, practices such as astrology and palmistry, which employ pseudo-science and pseudo-scientific terms, will become more popular. There are dozens of magazines that tell readers what the stars foretell about the week ahead; there are also millions of copies of birthday forecasts sold in the market.

No Guarantee of Truth

Pray for your Hindu friends that they will disavow such practices as divination and astrology. They know by experience that the predictions of the astrologer or the palm reader may or may not come true; with such doubtful results, why should they sell themselves to such practices? Why not trust someone who is steadfast and who has every concern for you? The Word of God tells us that Christ is *the* door: "I am the gate; whoever enters through me will be saved. He will come in and go out, and find pasture" (John 10:9). We need to walk by faith, not by sight (2 Corinthians 5:7). We should "make it our goal to please him, whether we are at home in the body or away from it" (2 Corinthians 5:9).

There is no guarantee that the diviner or astrologer tells the truth, the whole truth, and nothing but the truth. As the Word of God says, what is most important is the ultimate truth, and that we see it only partly now: "Now we see but a poor reflection as in a mirror; then we shall see face to face. Now I know in part; then I shall know fully, even as I am fully known" (1 Corinthians 13:12). There is a curtain between the future and us, and we should avoid the temptation to peer through it through the use of dubious processes. We must put our faith in Jesus, since His body was the curtain that was sacrificed for us. As the writer of Hebrews says,

> Therefore, brothers, since we have confidence to enter the Most Holy Place by the blood of Jesus, by a new and living way opened for us through the curtain, that is, his body, and since we have a great priest over the house of God, let us draw near to God with a sincere heart in full assurance of faith, having our hearts sprinkled to cleanse us from a guilty conscience

and having our bodies washed with pure water. Let us hold unswervingly to the hope we profess, for he who promised is faithful. (10:19–23)

WHY SHOULD WE BE AGAINST ASTROLOGY?

There is objection to divination and astrology for various reasons. First, as explained above, it is a question of faith. If we surrender our lives to the Lord Jesus Christ, there is no justification whatsoever in going after divination, for doing so betrays our trust in Jesus. Second, divination is often mechanical, using material objects and imputing to them divine power, giving a spiritual color to the material object. Third, more often than not, during subjective divination, the diviner allows himself to be possessed by, or assumes the personality of, the spirits. He makes himself a medium to receive and transmit messages, and there is no endorsement in the Word of God of trancing or the transfer of spiritual power from one object to another. It is clearly stated that the *prophets are in control of their spirits; they do not become or allow other spirits to enter them*. We are cautioned,

> The spirits of prophets are subject to the control of prophets. For God is not a God of disorder but of peace. (1 Corinthians 14:32–33)
> Dear friends, do not believe every spirit, but test the spirits to see whether they are from God, because many false prophets have gone out into the world. This is how you can recognize the Spirit of God: Every spirit that acknowledges that Jesus Christ has come in the flesh is from God, but every spirit that does not acknowledge Jesus is not from God. This is the spirit of the antichrist, which you have heard is coming and even now is already in the world. (1 John 4:1–3)

The dream of Pilate's wife (Matthew 27:19) confirms the early belief in the use of dreams as a means of divination, but we also are cautioned against Simon the sorcerer (Acts 8:9) and Elymas, the sorcerer of Cyprus:

> They traveled through the whole island until they came to Paphos. There they met a Jewish sorcerer and false prophet named Bar-Jesus, who was an attendant of the proconsul, Sergius Paulus. The proconsul, an intelligent man, sent for Bar-

nabas and Saul because he wanted to hear the word of God. But Elymas the sorcerer (for that is what his name means) opposed them and tried to turn the proconsul from the faith. Then Saul, who was also called Paul, filled with the Holy Spirit, looked straight at Elymas and said, "You are a child of the devil and an enemy of everything that is right! You are full of all kinds of deceit and trickery. Will you never stop perverting the right ways of the Lord? Now the hand of the Lord is against you. You are going to be blind, and for a time you will be unable to see the light of the sun" (Acts 13:6–11).

Consider also the following instance from the ministry of Paul:

> Once when we were going to the place of prayer, we were met by a slave girl who had a spirit by which she predicted the future. She earned a great deal of money for her owners by fortune-telling. This girl followed Paul and the rest of us, shouting, "These men are servants of the Most High God, who are telling you the way to be saved." She kept this up for many days. Finally Paul became so troubled that he turned around and said to the spirit, "In the name of Jesus Christ I command you to come out of her!" At that moment the spirit left her. (Acts 16:16–18)

This is a clear condemnation of divination using spirits. A similar condemnation for sorcery is found in Acts 19:19, when it was reported that the sorcerers brought their scrolls together and burned them while the Word prospered.

DIVINATION DISTRACTS OUR ATTENTION FROM GOD

The question is not whether the church authorizes divination and astrology; the question is whether such practices distract our attention to develop total faith in Jesus Christ. Divination in any form is giving prominence in our thought to forces outside of our Lord, and, hence, it should be avoided. The apostle Paul fought a relentless battle against the divination practices of those who claimed to be followers of Christ. He wrote,

> You foolish Galatians! Who has bewitched you? Before your very eyes Jesus was clearly portrayed as crucified. I would like to learn just one thing from you: Did you receive the

Spirit by observing the law? . . . After beginning with the Spirit, are you now trying to attain your goal by human effort? (Galatians 3:1–3)

This trend continued in the writings of the early church fathers, who warned the people against being curious of ungodly pursuits. Clearly, we must take caution, rejecting spiritual or material activities that do not honor God and that turn our eyes and hearts away from devotedness to Him.

SACRIFICE

9

Sacrifice refers to the action of giving something that one values for the goal of receiving something more valuable—to God, a god, a deity, a spiritual being, or the dead. *Sacrifice* also refers to the thing offered; while Hindus offer many kinds of sacrifices to their gods, the sacrifice is often an animal. Generally speaking, animal sacrifice is quite common among the lower classes of people, but this factor alone cannot be used to judge the social ranking of Hindus. There are well-known temples, frequented by upper-caste people, with gods considered by the Hindus to be very powerful, in which animal sacrifices are openly offered. Other things offered are vegetables, other foods, drink, incense, or precious objects. Offering of one's own hair from the head is also found among all Hindu groups.

In addition to sacrifices, Hindus make offerings to their gods on all occasions. Before they begin eating their food, they may offer it to their gods; before they put on a new garment, they may worship their gods and make the garment an offering. If some liquid is offered as sacrifice, libation (pouring liquid over the idols—water from "holy rivers," milk, scent, or oil, for example) is the generally adopted form.

Occasionally one hears about sacrifices offered in stealth. When mammoth constructions such as multi-story buildings or dams are undertaken, rumor spreads that some human sacrifice was performed to ensure that the process remains stable and safe. So Hindus make bloodless offerings and blood offerings, both long-held traditions within Hinduism.

One of the most troubling aspects of these sacrifices is that the sacrificer makes the offering with an expectation that through it the god or spirit will meet his desires. Sacrifices, then, often function as gifts to bribe the spiritual powers.

The destruction of the Jerusalem temple and the dispersal of the Jews resulted in the discontinuation of the sacrifices offered, though Jewish religious prayers even now include a request for the revival of the sacrifices. However, we see clearly in the Old Testament a move toward the abolition of sacrifices of various sorts. The offering of the soul, the outpouring of the broken spirit, the presentation of the meek mind, the sacrifice of the lips (Hosea 14:2), the meditations of the heart (Psalm 19:14)—these are acceptable to the Lord.

ANIMAL SACRIFICES IN THE OLD TESTAMENT

Your Hindu friend will certainly raise the issue of animal sacrifices as presented in the Old Testament; folk religious Hindus will find plenty of similarity between these sacrifices and those performed in their temples. The Old Testament *does* abound with instances of sacrifice; however, even there, importance is given to the motive of the sacrifice, the intent of the sacrificer, and how he or she looks at sacrifice from a spiritual perspective. There are also clear prohibitions against human sacrifice and sacrifices given to idols and false gods. Early in the Old Testament, we are told that to obey the Lord is better than any sacrifice (1 Samuel 15:22–23).

> But Samuel replied: "Does the LORD delight in burnt offerings and sacrifices as much as in obeying the voice of the LORD? To obey is better than sacrifice, and to heed is better than the fat of rams. For rebellion is like the sin of divination, and arrogance like the evil of idolatry."

Consider also the following verses.

> Sacrifice and offering you did not desire, but my ears you have pierced; burnt offerings and sin offerings you did not require. Then I said, "Here I am, I have come—it is written about me in the scroll. I desire to do your will, O my God; your law is within my heart" (Psalm 40:6–8).
> Do I eat the flesh of bulls or drink the blood of goats? Sacrifice thank offerings to God, fulfill your vows to the Most High, and call upon me in the day of trouble; I will deliver you, and you will honor me. (Psalm 50:13–15)

You do not delight in sacrifice, or I would bring it; you do not take pleasure in burnt offerings. The sacrifices of God are a broken spirit; a broken and contrite heart, O God, you will not despise. (Psalm 51:16–17)

The LORD detests the sacrifice of the wicked, but the prayer of the upright pleases him. (Proverbs 15:8)

Hear the word of the LORD, you rulers of Sodom; listen to the law of our God, you people of Gomorrah! "The multitude of your sacrifices—what are they to me?" says the LORD. "I have more than enough of burnt offerings, of rams and the fat of fattened animals; I have no pleasure in the blood of bulls and lambs and goats. When you come to appear before me, who has asked this of you, this trampling of my courts? Stop bringing meaningless offerings! Your incense is detestable to me. New Moons, Sabbaths and convocations—I cannot bear your evil assemblies. Your New Moon festivals and your appointed feasts my soul hates. They have become a burden to me; I am weary of bearing them. When you spread out your hands in prayer, I will hide my eyes from you; even if you offer many prayers, I will not listen" (Isaiah 1:10–15).

To do what is right and just is more acceptable to the LORD than sacrifice. (Proverbs 21:3)

For I desire mercy, not sacrifice, and acknowledgment of God rather than burnt offerings. (Hosea 6:6)

SACRIFICE IN THE NEW TESTAMENT

While Jesus was having dinner at Matthew's house, many tax collectors and "sinners" came and ate with him and his disciples. When the Pharisees saw this, they asked his disciples, "Why does your teacher eat with tax collectors and 'sinners'?" On hearing this, Jesus said, "It is not the healthy who need a doctor, but the sick. But go and learn what this means: 'I desire mercy, not sacrifice.' For I have not come to call the righteous, but sinners" (Matthew 9:10–13).

There is no difference, for all have sinned and fall short of the glory of God, and are justified freely by his grace through the redemption that came by Christ Jesus. God presented him as a sacrifice of atonement, through faith in his blood. He did this to demonstrate his justice, because in his forbearance he had left the sins committed beforehand unpunished—he did it to demonstrate his justice at the present time, so as to be just and the one who justifies those who have faith in Jesus. (Romans 3:22–26)

Be imitators of God, therefore, as dearly loved children and live a life of love, just as Christ loved us and gave himself up for us as a fragrant offering and sacrifice to God. (Ephesians 5:1–2)

Not that I am looking for a gift, but I am looking for what may be credited to your account. I have received full payment and even more; I am amply supplied, now that I have received from Epaphroditus the gifts you sent. They are a fragrant offering, an acceptable sacrifice, pleasing to God. (Philippians 4:17–18)

In fact, the law requires that nearly everything be cleansed with blood, and without the shedding of blood there is no forgiveness. It was necessary, then, for the copies of the heavenly things to be purified with these sacrifices, but the heavenly things themselves with better sacrifices than these. For Christ did not enter a man-made sanctuary that was only a copy of the true one; he entered heaven itself, now to appear for us in God's presence. Nor did he enter heaven to offer himself again and again, the way the high priest enters the Most Holy Place every year with blood that is not his own. Then Christ would have had to suffer many times since the creation of the world. But now he has appeared once for all at the end of the ages to do away with sin by the sacrifice of himself. (Hebrews 9:22–26)

First he said, "Sacrifices and offerings, burnt offerings and sin offerings you did not desire, nor were you pleased with them" (although the law required them to be made). Then he said, "Here I am, I have come to do your will." He sets aside the first to establish the second. And by that will, we have been made holy through the sacrifice of the body of Jesus Christ once for all . . ." (Hebrews 10:8–10).

Day after day every priest stands and performs his religious duties; again and again he offers the same sacrifices, which can never take away sins. But when this priest [Jesus] had offered for all time one sacrifice for sins, he sat down at the right hand of God. Since that time he waits for his enemies to be made his footstool, because by one sacrifice he has made perfect forever those who are being made holy. (Hebrews 10:11–14)

And where these have been forgiven, there is no longer any sacrifice for sin. (Hebrews 10:18)

He [Jesus Christ] is the atoning sacrifice for our sins, and not only for ours but also for the sins of the whole world. (1 John 2:2)

From these verses it is clear that the only sacrifice God wants from us is our faith in Him as Lord and Savior, along with a holy life. Jesus Christ sacrificed himself once for all to atone for our sins and to reconcile us with the Father. Any other sacrifice offered to Him or to other gods, spiritual beings, or men is against the Word of God. Moreover, sacrifices and offerings made to gods, spiritual beings, or men are in the realm of a continuing business transaction; there is nothing spiritual about it, for it is more a matter of convenience for the sacrificer and the recipient of the sacrifice.

Once we begin to offer sacrifices to spiritual beings, there is never an end to it. For anything and everything we want from these gods, spiritual beings, or men, we are required to offer sacrifices. We are entrapped and cannot liberate ourselves, because it is in the interest of these gods, spiritual beings, or men that we are always bound to them. Over time the practice of sacrifice to gods, spiritual beings, or men will become a curse.

Apart from this fact, sacrifices and offerings drain the scarce resources of worshipers' families. There is no end to the craving of the human heart or to the lusts of these spiritual beings. Sacrifices to gods are manmade, based on some sort of divining the will and desire of spiritual beings, whereas the form and function of sacrifice both in the Old and New Testaments are God-ordained. God has *removed* the guilt offering of individual sinners as the basis of atonement (Old Testament) and has offered His Son as the one-time guilt offering so that we may live holy lives through faith in Jesus Christ. We accept the will of God as the basis of life, and we recognize its sovereignty over us.

SOCIAL SOLIDARITY—NO EXCUSE FOR SACRIFICE

Unfortunately, there is still some confusion in the minds of those who would like to contextualize the gospel in diverse cultures and to make the gospel "relevant and right" for newly converted Christian communities and individuals. Some have argued that offering sacrifices in the traditional way of the pre-Christian community may help social solidarity; it is alleged that such sacrifices become occasions for the community to gather and show their unity. Again, we must understand that this kind of sacrifice is not what God wants from us. If our *heart* is not pure, nothing else can help us. There are other acceptable ways to express the culture and community solidarity and allegiance: communal gatherings to honor people, preservation of the best cultural traditions that foster neighborly love, retention of ethnic and linguistic identities, developing indigenous art forms, or carrying out need-filling social activities.

The new Christian from the folk religious Hindu background may show a tendency to fall back on various sacrifices. In our desire to seek immediate results and benefits, we may be tempted to seek other powers, convincing our hearts that we would do this only once and only for this immediate exigency. To wean ourselves from such temptations is possible only if we hold firmly to the Word of God.

CHAPTER

SPIRIT POSSESSION AND SPIRITISM

10

I want to briefly discuss the various parts of humanity as created by God, in order that we might come to a better understanding of what it means to be dealing with spirit possession. Body, mind, soul, and spirit are often referred to when we contemplate our composition. While "body" is rather easily understood as the external form—a concrete object that decays when a person dies—the meanings of "mind," "soul," and "spirit" often overlap, and we get confused by the interchangeability of the terms in several contexts.

The mind is a concept with which we are all familiar, yet it is difficult to describe exactly what the mind is. At one level of meaning, the mind is identified with memory as the state of remembering or being remembered. At another level of meaning, it refers to the inclinations, intentions, desires, wishes, and purposes we have. The mind is often considered to be that which reasons, the sum total of the conscious states of the individual. The mind is a part of the living organism: When a person dies, his mind, in its active role, dies with him; we do not view the mind as existing after death.

Among Hindus, some materialistic schools of thought consider man to be only physical matter, a belief similar to so-called "scientific" explanations. However, most systems of philosophy within Hinduism suggest that the soul is separated from the body after death and that the dead person may be reborn in another form. (See chapter two.) The soul may fly like a bird to the world of ancestors (called *pitrloka*) or to the world of the gods (called *devaloka*). Again, the ultimate goal of a Hindu, through transmigration based on the consequences of his or her karma, is to get enveloped by the Universal Soul and be part of it; salvation, supposedly, is the realization that there is no distinction between the individual soul and the Universal Soul.

SOUL AND SPIRIT IN THE BIBLE

The distinction the Bible makes between soul and spirit is not clearly found in the Hindu belief system. When the soul leaves the body and is reborn according to the consequences of karma, the earlier body has been lost upon death, and the soul assumes a new physical body through its rebirth. This physical body may be a plant, animal, insect, bird, or any creature; each one is possessed with a distinct soul, and the soul, through its births and rebirths, does its best to get liberated from the shackles of the physical body and to become merged with the Universal Soul.

The New Testament brings some subtle changes to our view of soul, raising questions such as "What good will it be for a man if he gains the whole world, yet forfeits his soul? Or what can a man give in exchange for his soul?" (Matthew 16:26; see also Mark 8:36 and Luke 9:25).

Any topical Bible or concordance will show that references to individual spirits and the Spirit of God are abundant in the Old Testament, but the New Testament is the book of the Holy Spirit. Also note that the apostle Paul does not *define* "spirit," but he is greatly interested in the *working* of the spirit.

While there is no explicitly stated distinction between soul and spirit, the Bible uses the word *soul* for the flesh/spirit connection of man. We read in Genesis 2:7 (KJV), "The LORD God formed man of the dust of the ground, and breathed into his nostrils the breath of life, and man became a living soul."

The soul is abstract, relating to the body at one end and to the spiritual dimension at the other; the soul is related to the body even as it is the window to the spiritual realm. *The soul is not identical to the spirit*—it is our spirit that is in communion with the Spirit of God, and it is man's spirit within him that knows Him best. No one knows the thoughts of God except His Spirit:

The man without the Spirit does not accept the things that come from the Spirit of God, for they are foolishness to him, and he cannot understand them, because they are spiritually discerned. (1 Corinthians 2:14)

The wind blows wherever it pleases. You hear its sound, but you cannot tell where it comes from or where it is going. So it is with everyone born of the Spirit. (John 3:8)

God is spirit, and his worshipers must worship in spirit and in truth. (John 4:24)

We believe that all individuals have their own souls; most theologians suggest that God creates a new soul for each human being, while a few believe that the soul is transmitted along with the body by the parents. Still a smaller number suggest that the soul preexisted the birth of the individual, that God has created all souls beforehand, and that these souls undergo many embodiments. This last view is attributed to Origen (c. 185–254), some of whose teachings led to speculation that he was a heretic.

The resurrection of the body is dealt with by Paul in 1 Corinthians 15:35–53. Also, he tells us that our spirit is in a struggle not against flesh and blood, but against the powers of this dark world and against the spiritual forces of evil in the heavenly realms. We can win the battle only with the sword of the Spirit, which is the Word of God (Ephesians 6:17).

Finally, we must remember that the distinction between soul and spirit is more or less a distinctive revelation of God that often is not recognized in other religions. Hindus who practice or seek spirit possession for various purposes, such as divination, exploit the thin bridge between the soul and spirit of man to flood his soul with all kinds of spirits. Even though it is difficult to make the distinction between soul and spirit, the Word of God clearly says that each has a distinct identity, recognizable only with the help of God's revelation through His Word:

> The word of God is living and active. Sharper than any double-edged sword, it penetrates even to dividing soul and spirit, joints and marrow; it judges the thoughts and attitudes of the heart. Nothing in all creation is hidden from God's sight. Everything is uncovered and laid bare before the eyes of him to whom we must give account. (Hebrews 4:12–13)

What Is Spirit Possession?

Spirit possession is a state of consciousness induced in a person by an alien spirit, demon, or deity; another personality takes control, and the person is often not fully conscious when such a takeover occurs. In spirit possession, the person possessed shows a dramatic change in physical appearance, actions, voice, and manner, and frequently he or she remembers nothing of the possession. Behavior varies according to the kind and number of spirits that take possession.

Spirit possession is a common phenomenon among Hindus. In some cases, family traditions require that someone from the family, preferably the firstborn son or daughter, become the temple priest or shaman, and this is accomplished through a demonstration of spirit possession. The person suddenly goes into a trance as an involuntary act and is beside himself during the rituals performed in the temple. There is always an expectation that the spirits will descend on the firstborn in the village-temple-priest's family; this expectation creates a welcome atmosphere to receive the spirits. Subsequent possessions are usually induced through the inhalation of incense or fumes, ingestion of drugs, partaking in animal sacrifice and drinking the blood of the victim, or through bombardment of noise such as drumming, dancing, or incantation of repetitive chants.

The possessed persons perform uncanny feats, such as walking over burning coals, piercing themselves with skewers and pins, self-flagellation, chest-beating that leads to bleeding, carrying heavy loads of stone or other objects, drinking the blood of animals sacrificed, heavy consumption of alcohol, and so on. While this is not considered harmful to the possessed, there is yet another case where individuals may be involuntarily possessed, this being revealed through sicknesses of various sorts, depression, and other such psychic manifestations. Hindus often assume this latter category to be a fit case for exorcism. Spirit possession, whether in a priest or in ordinary persons, becomes a public spectacle. People gather around and view the entire proceedings of exorcism and spirit possession with awe and fear. Such exorcism can be terrifying to the spectators because the possessed one is subjected to all kinds of torture at the hands of the exorcist: she may be driven around, beaten, or asked to perform acts that inflict harm upon her body. Sometimes the spirits may be induced to leave through offerings of food or animal sacrifice.

EXORCISM

Deliverance and healing from the clutches of spirit possession, which has been doing damage for thousands of years, is one of the neediest areas in the Hindu religion. Even the ancient sacred Hindu texts, such as *Atharva-veda*, list the spells that should be used for exorcising spirits. Hindu gods are called upon to command spirits to go away and to ward off pests; gods are requested to burn spirits and even crush the bones of the sorcerers who allow spirits to come and enter persons. Charms have been suggested to overcome the influence of demons, rivals, magicians, wizards, and enemies. Unfortunately, spirit possession is an important factor in becoming a village temple priest or shaman. So the religious practices encourage spirit possession at one level and try to exorcise spirits at another level. This is like trying to drive away the spirits using the spirits; as Jesus said, "How can Satan drive out Satan?" (Mark 3:23).

Hindu women have always been spirit-possessed in greater numbers than Hindu men. Traumatic life experiences open doors to seek the help of spirits, which in turn cause their own trauma. Since Hinduism does encourage spirit possession, and since many Hindus seek the help of spirits for divination, healing, and material prosperity, they are more easily subjected to the evil designs of Satan.

If you know a Hindu friend who is in need of help, you may divert him from seeking help from spirits by showing him some of David's psalms and suggesting he read them and meditate on them. David underwent unspeakable suffering in his life, but he held on to the promises of God, even putting into song how God fortifies against all adversity. Anyone in need can identify with the psalms of David.

When we know someone is suffering from depression, we might offer a short prayer of encouragement. Even offering a Bible portion, to a Hindu whom we have come to know well, may be well received. I have known many Hindus who were willing to read or meditate on the Word of God because every attempt to improve their condition within their own religious traditions had failed.

Hindu exorcism is really not exorcism at all; it does not lead to a permanent cure but is only an attempt to replace one set of evil spirits with another. Whereas driving out demons in the name of Jesus is annihilation of the authority of the demons over the person or persons they possessed.

The animist uses one evil spirit against another evil spirit. Some accused Jesus of doing this, saying, "By Beelzebub, the prince of demons, he is driving out demons." Jesus answered,

> Any kingdom divided against itself will be ruined, and a house divided against itself will fall. If Satan is divided against himself, how can his kingdom stand? I say this because you claim that I drive out demons by Beelzebub. Now if I drive out demons by Beelzebub, by whom do your followers drive them out? So then, they will be your judges. But if I drive out demons by the finger of God, then the kingdom of God has come to you. (Luke 11:15, 17–20)

THE WORD OF GOD, SPIRIT POSSESSION, AND EXORCISM

How do we respond to spirit possession? How do we deal with exorcism? The Word of God tells us that God is Spirit (John 4:24), and that He has left us His Holy Spirit. The Bible recognizes that there are real spiritual beings and that there is a continuing struggle between the angelic forces and evil spirits in the spiritual realm. Satan is a tempter of people (Genesis 3:1–5; Matthew 4:1–11; 1 Thessalonians 3:5), the adversary and slanderer of God. He is a distinct malevolent spiritual being who from the start has worked against God's plans.

First John 3:8 says, "The devil has been sinning from the beginning." In Revelation 12:9 we read that the ancient serpent called the devil or Satan leads the whole world astray. He rules the minds of all unbelievers and is called the god of this age who "has blinded the minds of unbelievers, so that they cannot see the light of the gospel of the glory of Christ, who is the image of God" (2 Corinthians 4:4). He is also called "the ruler of the kingdom of the air" (Ephesians 2:2) who tries to ensnare the new believer to make him his captive:

> He [an overseer in the church] must not be a recent convert, or he may become conceited and fall under the same judgment as the devil. He must also have a good reputation with outsiders, so that he will not fall into disgrace and into the devil's trap. (1 Timothy 3:6–7)
> Those who oppose him [the Lord's servant] he must gently instruct, in the hope that God will grant them repentance

leading them to a knowledge of the truth, and that they will come to their senses and escape from the trap of the devil, who has taken them captive to do his will. (2 Timothy 2:25–26)

Satan himself masquerades as an angel of light. It is not surprising, then, if his servants masquerade as servants of righteousness (2 Corinthians 11:14–15). He prowls "like a roaring lion looking for someone to devour" (1 Peter 5:8).

The good news is that Jesus came to this world to overcome the archenemy of God: "The reason the Son of God appeared was to destroy the devil's work" (1 John 3:8). Jesus came to claim victory over death for all of us: "Since the children have flesh and blood, he [Jesus] too shared in their humanity so that by his death he might destroy him who holds the power of death—that is, the devil—and free those who all their lives were held in slavery by their fear of death" (Hebrews 2:14–15).

In Colossians 1:13–14 we read, "For he has rescued us from the dominion of darkness and brought us into the kingdom of the Son he loves, in whom we have redemption, the forgiveness of sins."

And in Colossians 2:15 we are told, "Having disarmed the powers and authorities, he made a public spectacle of them, triumphing over them by the cross." Thus victory is already ours, and we need to appropriate it by faith in Jesus Christ. Ephesians 6:10–18 invites us to put on the full armor of God so that we can take our stand against the devil's schemes.

While the victory is ours in Jesus' name, we must recognize that exorcism is not an end in itself:

> When an evil spirit comes out of a man, it goes through arid places seeking rest and does not find it. Then it says, "I will return to the house I left." When it arrives, it finds the house unoccupied, swept clean and put in order. Then it goes and takes with it seven other spirits more wicked than itself, and they go in and live there. And the final condition of that man is worse than the first. (Matthew 12:43–45)

Note that the house (the person) was kept clean and put in order and yet the evil spirits were emboldened to return in strength. Cleanliness in the natural, *without the armor of God's Word in the heart*, is an easy place for the spirits to return. So it is important for us to give the Gospel to those for whom we have prayed and whom the Spirit of God has delivered from evil spirits. The place the spirits occupied must be filled up with God's Spirit.

THE POWER OF GOD IS GIVEN TO US

Power is given to all of us, the disciples and children of God, to drive out demons in Jesus' name (Mark 16:17). When Jesus sent out the twelve, "they went out and preached that people should repent. They drove out many demons and anointed many sick people with oil and healed them" (Mark 6:12–13). However, this authority is not given for our personal glory. Jesus said, "I have given you authority to trample on snakes and scorpions and to overcome all the power of the enemy; nothing will harm you. However, do not rejoice that the spirits submit to you, but rejoice that your names are written in heaven" (Luke 10:19–20).

FAITH IS NECESSARY

Jesus taught that we must have faith in order to be effective in seeing demons cast out. When a boy was possessed, having seizures and falling into fire or water, suffering greatly, the disciples of Jesus could not heal him, but Jesus did:

> Then the disciples came to Jesus in private and asked, "Why couldn't we drive it out?" He replied, "Because you have so little faith. I tell you the truth, if you have faith as small as a mustard seed, you can say to this mountain, 'Move from here to here' and it will move. Nothing will be impossible for you" (Matthew 17:19–20).

FASTING AND PRAYER

Some demons can only be driven out through prayer and fasting:

> So they brought him. When the spirit saw Jesus, it immediately threw the boy into a convulsion. He fell to the ground and rolled around, foaming at the mouth. Jesus asked the boy's father, "How long has he been like this?" "From childhood," he answered. "It has often thrown him into fire or water to kill him. But if you can do anything, take pity on us and help us." " 'If you can'?" said Jesus. "Everything is pos-

sible for him who believes." . . . The spirit shrieked, convulsed him violently and came out. The boy looked so much like a corpse that many said, "He's dead." But Jesus took him by the hand and lifted him to his feet, and he stood up. After Jesus had gone indoors, his disciples asked him privately, "Why couldn't we drive it out?" He replied, "This kind can come out only by prayer" (Mark 9:20–23, 26–29).

Day after day they seek me out; they seem eager to know my ways, as if they were a nation that does what is right and has not forsaken the commands of its God. They ask me for just decisions and seem eager for God to come near them. "Why have we fasted," they say, "and you have not seen it? Why have we humbled ourselves, and you have not noticed?" Yet on the day of your fasting, you do as you please and exploit all your workers. Your fasting ends in quarreling and strife, and in striking each other with wicked fists. You cannot fast as you do today and expect your voice to be heard on high. Is this the kind of fast I have chosen, only a day for a man to humble himself? Is it only for bowing one's head like a reed and for lying on sackcloth and ashes? Is that what you call a fast, a day acceptable to the LORD? Is not this the kind of fasting I have chosen: to loose the chains of injustice and untie the cords of the yoke, to set the oppressed free and break every yoke? Is it not to share your food with the hungry and to provide the poor wanderer with shelter—when you see the naked, to clothe him, and not to turn away from your own flesh and blood? (Isaiah 58:2–7)

POSSESSION BY MULTIPLE SPIRITS

A person may be possessed by a multitude of spirits. In exorcisms that I have seen, the possessed often lists the names of spirits tormenting her. Sometimes she may not know the names of the spirits and say that she is possessed by a horde of spirits. We see this in one of the incidents presented in the Gospels.

When Jesus stepped ashore, he was met by a demon-possessed man from the town. For a long time this man had not worn clothes or lived in a house, but had lived in the tombs. When he saw Jesus, he cried out and fell at his feet, shouting at the top of his voice, "What do you want with me, Jesus, Son of the Most High God? I beg you, don't torture me!" For Jesus had commanded the evil spirit to come out of the man. Many times it had seized him, and though he was chained hand and foot and kept under guard, he had broken his chains and had been driven by the demon into solitary places. Jesus asked him, "What is your name?" "Legion," he replied, because many demons had gone into him. (Luke 8:27–30)

Note that the demons do recognize the Son of God and His authority over everyone, including them.

God's healing power is available to us *all* the time. The synagogue ruler was furious that on the Sabbath Jesus healed a woman who was crippled by a spirit for eighteen years:

> "There are six days for work. So come and be healed on those days, not on the Sabbath." The Lord answered him, "You hypocrites! Doesn't each of you on the Sabbath untie his ox or donkey from the stall and lead it out to give it water? Then should not this woman, a daughter of Abraham, whom Satan has kept bound for eighteen long years, be set free on the Sabbath day from what bound her?" (Luke 13:14–16)

TRUE EXORCISM IS NOT AN EXCHANGE BUT A CHANGE

In Hinduism, exorcism operates as a trade, using manmade techniques to drive out evil spirits. They seek the help of other spirits to drive away the spirit inhabiting the individuals, but hardly any attempt is made to fill the vacuum created by the removal of the evil spirits. The spirits are engaged and enticed to leave the individual's body through offerings or bribes. Sometimes physical violence is resorted to in this process.

While we do not deny the existence and the influence of spiritual beings, we must also caution that such steps do not lead to a cure of the body and soul of the individual. Prayer in Jesus' name, rather than praying to other spirits, is the effective answer for spirit possession. No one should borrow the methods of exorcism from folk religious Hinduism. Fasting, prayer, and reading the Word of God must fill the life of one whose ministry is to the spirit-possessed.

Spiritism—Communication With the Spirits

Spiritism is different from spirit possession in that it is consulting the spirits. Spiritism is a phenomenon of the educated classes among the Hindus, the practitioners of which believe in the possibility of communicating with the spirits of the dead. Through this communication, they desire to receive messages from the dead for the benefit of the living.

Spiritism has a great attraction for the bereaved family who wants advice from the dead, especially to be certain the dead hold no grudges against them. They are not satisfied with fond memories; they want to hear the voice of their dead loved one and to feel and to touch him or her. A retired Supreme Court judge in India often tells of his spiritist encounters with his dead wife, his face glowing as he speaks.

The Spirit Enters the Body of a Living Person

The spirit, upon the death of the individual, is detached from the body and becomes independent. The spirit is believed to have enormous powers in this independence. It can enter another body and use that body to communicate with other spirits and living beings. But the bodies must be receptive to the entry of the independent spirit. Spiritism is possible only when a body is willing to receive the spirit and to act as a medium. Mediumship is rare, but individuals all over the world have accomplished this and practice their "trade" with some success.

Even now such practices are observed to a limited degree, especially among those who desperately want to talk to their dead. Mediums are now called psychics in the Western world. People are attracted to spiritism out of curiosity and then become slaves to it. The spirits that enable these encounters to happen are under the control of the devil.

To draw an even greater following to spiritism, there are a number who fraudulently claim medium status. Fraud is always a distinct possibility when people search for "spiritual" encounters for personal ends and personal profit. Remember the folly of Simon the Samaritan sorcerer:

When the apostles in Jerusalem heard that Samaria had

accepted the word of God, they sent Peter and John to them. When they arrived, they prayed for them that they might receive the Holy Spirit, because the Holy Spirit had not yet come upon any of them; they had simply been baptized into the name of the Lord Jesus. Then Peter and John placed their hands on them, and they received the Holy Spirit. When Simon saw that the Spirit was given at the laying on of the apostles' hands, he offered them money and said, "Give me also this ability so that everyone on whom I lay my hands may receive the Holy Spirit" (Acts 8:14–19).

The Word of God commands us: " 'Do not turn to mediums or seek out spiritists, for you will be defiled by them. I am the LORD your God' " (Leviticus 19:31). Modern spiritism cloaks itself with terms from psychology and other so-called sciences, and modern man is easily deceived because of the terminology. The mysterious happenings add color to the entire performance, but in the end, the customer risks losing his soul as well as his money.

MAGIC AND ANCESTOR WORSHIP

11

People in industrially advanced societies often pretend not to have any faith in magic, which they consider superstition. For them, "magic" usually refers to the sleight of hand performance that serves as entertainment. The educated among Hindus frequently take the same position, but when it comes to worshiping their gurus, magic begins to play a prominent role. Gurus are known to have magical powers through which it is believed they are able to solve the problems of their devotees. For folk religious Hindus, magic is more or less synonymous with religion; they seek magical demonstration and are convinced of the truthfulness of a religious experience if there is something magical about it.

In Hinduism, a magician is someone who uses supernatural power to work wonders, not someone (such as in America) who performs illusionary tricks for optical entertainment. Hindus seek the help of such magicians to solve their individual and family problems, for it is thought that only a magician can find out the reason for a persisting disease or a cycle of calamity that has befallen a person or group, and only a magician can reverse fortune or ward off evil forces. Hindus seek the help of magicians for many different reasons: to make a woman fall in love, to receive elixirs to rejuvenate themselves, or to avenge defeat, to name a few.

REASONS FOR THE DECLINE OF MAGIC

In society as a whole, there has been a recent decline in faith in magic. One reason may be that people can control their environment more easily than in the past. The development of the "scientific temperament" and the lessons of the history of Europe have resulted in greater confidence in upward progress and less dependence on magic. Over the centuries, the emergence of the Protestant faith, which focused more on economic and literacy growth, has been a factor, as well as the spread of education, easy transportation and communication, modern means of production and distribution, the growth of statistics as a scientific discipline, the emergence of empirical psychology, and developments in the field of medicine—all of these have led to a greater confidence in humankind rather than in forces that cannot be scientifically proven.

Hindu society, however, shows a return to the use of magic even as it modernizes itself. If people in the villages with little or no education seek the services of magicians to meet their material and spiritual needs, people in higher economic levels with accelerated education and social and political power seek the help of well-renowned magicians or gurus to secure their position, wealth, and health.

Hindu Magic and Alchemy

For centuries Hindus have been interested in seeking magical powers through special disciplines such as yoga, believing that it could be obtained through concentration of the will. They seek clairvoyance and telepathy; some would like to remember their former lives and develop knowledge of future lives, ultimately obtaining liberation from karma through such disciplines.

A classical text entitled *Yoga Sutras*, written by Patanjali around the second century B.C., lists a number of powers that an individual can acquire through the practice of yoga. Wish fulfillment, levitation, creating objects, mass illusions, feeding on air, and transforming oneself into other forms of life or objects are some examples.

Magicians may adopt natural, sympathetic, black, or white magic. In *natural* magic, herbs are used to influence the spirits; potions are made that impact those who take them. In *sympathetic* magic, it is assumed that an enemy may be made to suffer by performing operations on a wax or cloth doll or image that represents the enemy. A man's hair, nail clippings, articles of clothing, sand under his feet, his shadow, or his name may be used against him. But the most popular magic is *black* magic. The purpose of black magic is to cause harm to others, whereas the purpose of *white* magic is to protect oneself from the harm that may be caused by others and to coerce the spirits to work for the benefit of the person who has sought the help of the magician.

There is a clear distinction made between prayer and magic. Magic compels the spirits and gods, whereas prayer persuades them.

WHY DO WE REJECT MAGIC?

The Word of God takes a clear stand against magic and magical practices:

> Let no one be found among you who sacrifices his son or daughter in the fire, who practices divination or sorcery, interprets omens, engages in witchcraft, or casts spells, or who is a medium or spiritist or who consults the dead. Anyone who does these things is detestable to the LORD. (Deuteronomy 18:10–12)

The power of magic and magicians is clearly inferior to the power of God. The prophet Daniel was ten times better than all the magicians and enchanters in Nebuchadnezzar's palace in every matter of wisdom and understanding (Daniel 1:20). Pharaoh's magicians failed to interpret his dreams, and while they worked magical acts (Exodus 7:11–12, 22; 8:7, 18), they failed miserably to match the power of God: "But when the magicians tried to produce gnats by their secret arts, they could not. And the gnats were on men and animals. The magicians said to Pharaoh, 'This is the finger of God' " (Exodus 8:18–19).

FALSEHOOD OF MAGIC

The Word of God includes necromancy (consulting the spirits of the dead), exorcism, shaking arrows, inspecting the entrails of animals, divination, sorcery, astrology, soothsaying, divining by rods, and witchcraft as part of magical arts. The Old Testament attests to the fact that both the Israelites and their neighboring communities willingly sought after magicians and that God was fully against this (Micah 5:12–13). Wearing magic charms, amulets, earrings, and magic bands was likewise condemned:

Now, son of man, set your face against the daughters of your people who prophesy out of their own imagination. Prophesy against them and say, "This is what the Sovereign LORD says: 'Woe to the women who sew magic charms on all their wrists and make veils of various lengths for their heads in order to ensnare people' " (Ezekiel 13:17–18).

MAGIC WILL CONTINUE

The book of Revelation predicts the continuation and survival of magic arts even after awful manifestations of God's wrath:

The rest of mankind that were not killed by these plagues still did not repent of the work of their hands; they did not stop worshiping demons, and idols of gold, silver, bronze, stone and wood—idols that cannot see or hear or walk. Nor did they repent of their murders, their magic arts, their sexual immorality or their thefts. (Revelation 9:20–21)

The second death includes "the cowardly, the unbelieving, the vile, the murderers, the sexually immoral, those who practice magic arts, the idolaters and all liars—their place will be in the fiery lake of burning sulfur" (Revelation 21:8). Jesus proclaims that at the end those who practice magic arts are sure to be left out of the kingdom of God:

Blessed are those who wash their robes, that they may have the right to the tree of life and may go through the gates into the city. Outside are the dogs, those who practice magic arts, the sexually immoral, the murderers, the idolaters and everyone who loves and practices falsehood. (Revelation 22:14–15)

THE CASE OF SIMON MAGNUS

The story of Simon Magnus illustrates how people may confuse the power of God and magical powers drawn from other sources. People of faith seek the power of God for His glory, whereas others look at it only as a neutral power that could be manipulated to meet their ends (Acts 8:9–23). Simon thought the power of God was obtainable at will and could be bought, just as magical powers are obtained by propitiating the spirits through offerings of various sorts. He also thought that he could use the power of God at his will, just as he could manipulate the powers of magic.

The ministry of Jesus, as well as that of the disciples, is full of miracles, yet people often misread the miracles as magical acts. The power of Jesus over diseases and spirits is given to Paul and to all the believing children of God, and they may heal the sick by the power of the name of Jesus. But this does not mean that the name of Jesus is an incantation that can be used and manipulated at will, as are other incantations used by magicians.

MAGIC AND MIRACLES

This takes us to the question of the relationship between magic and miracles: are these one and the same? To begin with, the miracles attested to in the Bible are not conjuring acts like magic; they were performed as part of the work of God in history for His people's salvation and with the understanding and acceptance of His message.

A miracle is not a mere performance; it is a sign, a symbol that stands for something else. A miracle is extraordinary and remarkable in itself; however, its importance does not lie in its remarkableness but in its function as a message from God. An ordinary magical act attracts attention to *it* and does not go beyond—a magical act is neutral. A miracle from God is always for the good of all, "for the common good" (1 Corinthians 12:7).

In the Old Testament, miracles are associated more with the deliverance of the Israelite nation and the fulfillment of God's promise against all adversity, including sins committed by the people. Another major occasion for miracles was when the prophets were used by God to give signs and work wonders. Miracles demonstrated God's saving power and faithfulness on behalf of His people.

NEW TESTAMENT MIRACLES

Scholars classify the miracles found in the New Testament into three categories: healing, exorcism, and miracles of nature. While healings and exorcisms were performed in the ministry of Jesus as well as the disciples, it was only Jesus who performed the miracles of nature (such as turning water into wine, stilling the storm on the sea, and the multiplication of food to feed crowds). It appears that the miracles of nature that Jesus performed are in a special category, because no structural outline of the process can be gleaned from them. Hindu gurus often claim that they will perform miracles of nature, but in reality such occurrences are reported only in mythology.

Miracles do happen every day. Faith is required *of* those for whom they are performed (Mark 9:22–24; Acts 14:9), and faith is required in those *through* whom they are performed (Matthew 17:20; 21:21; John 14:12; Acts 3:16; 4:30; 6:8).

Miracles are often demanded by unbelievers (Matthew 12:38–39; 16:1; Luke 11:16, 29; 23:8). The Bible shows how alleged miracles are performed by magicians (Exodus 7:10–12, 22; 8:7) or by other impostors (Matthew 7:22), and also that miracles may be performed through the powers of evil (2 Thessalonians 2:9; Revelation 16:14), even in support of false religions (Deuteronomy 13:1–3). Miracles may be worked by false christs (Matthew 24:24) and by false prophets (1 Samuel 28:7–14).

It is perhaps noteworthy that Jesus never produced a miracle ("a sign") at the whim of unbelievers. People who demand such evidence would not believe even if many such miracles were produced (Matthew 12:38–39; Mark 8:11–12). Hindu gurus, on the other hand, make it a point to generate "miracles" to impress the persons who visit them to seek their help.

Magicians in animistic societies create a deadly fear of themselves and of their art among the people; for instance, they often carry a skull. Many stories are told as to how the individuals obtain their magical powers. Often these accounts revolve around human sacrifice, especially of the firstborn child, offered to the magical power by the aspiring magician. The practice is secretive, anti-social, and often involves trickery.

ANCESTOR WORSHIP—NOT A RELIGION

Ancestor worship is worship of deceased kinsmen. This is different from the rites for the dead and beliefs about the dead in general. The reference to kinship is very important in ancestor worship.

When I was a small boy, my father used to take me to the riverside on an "auspicious" new moon day in February/March to make offerings to the *pitr* (forefathers) through the good offices of a Brahman priest, who would set up his "shop" in the morning and recite Sanskrit *slokas* (verses) in honor of the dead forefathers of the worshiper and offer them uncooked rice, vegetables, or pieces of new cloth. The priest is given an offering for the services he renders, and he is allowed to take the other offerings made to the dead forefathers as well. This was done once a year, and the forefathers were generally forgotten until the following year.

Ancestor worship begins with the worship of the recently dead parents and grandparents, and it is then extended to a group of ancestors. It is required that every pious Hindu offers rituals to his ancestors so that they are satisfied and will live in peace in the world beyond. Ancestor worship does not include dead or stillborn children, miscarriages, or abortions, nor does it include those who die before marriage. These categories of people are to be appeased in other forms of worship.

IS ANCESTOR WORSHIP FOUND IN THE WORD OF GOD?

Is there any specific reference to ancestor worship in the Bible? There is a clear indication that giving offerings to the ancestors was practiced. In Deuteronomy 26:14, the tithe-giver was commanded to assure and say, "I have not eaten any of the sacred portion while I was in mourning, nor have I removed any of it while I was unclean, nor have I offered any of it to the dead."

There is reference to the burning of incense for the dead in Jeremiah 34:5: "You will die peacefully. As people made a funeral fire in honor of your fathers, the former kings who preceded you, so they will make a fire in your honor and lament, 'Alas, O master!' "

In Ezekiel 43:7–9 we read a strong condemnation of the practice of worshiping the dead (kings):

> Son of man, this is the place of my throne and the place for the soles of my feet. This is where I will live among the Israelites forever. The house of Israel will never again defile my holy name—neither they nor their kings—by their prostitution and the lifeless idols of their kings at their high places. When they placed their threshold next to my threshold and their doorposts beside my doorposts, with only a wall between me and them, they defiled my holy name by their detestable practices. So I destroyed them in my anger. Now let them put away from me their prostitution and the lifeless idols of their

SHARING YOUR FAITH WITH A HINDU

kings, and I will live among them forever.

Isaiah 65:1–4 is a powerful rebuke of the practice of according sanctity to the graves of family members:

> I revealed myself to those who did not ask for me; I was found by those who did not seek me. To a nation that did not call on my name, I said, "Here am I, here am I." All day long I have held out my hands to an obstinate people, who walk in ways not good, pursuing their own imaginations—a people who continually provoke me to my very face, offering sacrifices in gardens and burning incense on altars of brick; who sit among the graves and spend their nights keeping secret vigil; who eat the flesh of pigs, and whose pots hold broth of unclean meat.

Consider once again Isaiah 8:19: "When men tell you to consult mediums and spiritists, who whisper and mutter, should not a people inquire of their God? Why consult the dead on behalf of the living?"

A CHRISTIAN RESPONSE TO ANCESTOR WORSHIP

How do we as Christians respond to ancestor worship? At the outset, I would like to point out that ancestor worship is not based solely upon respect and deference for dead family members. *This is not rejected in Christian thought: The Bible commands us to honor and obey the wisdom of our parents and elders.* However, going beyond showing respect and obedience to worshiping them is against the Word of God. Honoring the dead in an excessive manner by setting up images, performing rituals, and making offerings of various kinds to them all indicate that some kind of idol worship is involved. Certainly it is obvious that we as Christians should not indulge in or approve of this.

TRADITION AND SUPERSTITION

12

Many Hindus consider Hinduism to be their "own" religion, as fundamentalist Hindu political and social groups encourage young people to think that nationalism and Hinduism are one and the same. Christianity, in contrast, is portrayed to them as a foreign religion, brought into India by those from other lands. However, there are groups of people, politicians and historians, who claim that the Aryans, who migrated from Europe thousands of years ago, brought Hinduism with them. A slow but steady miscegenation took place both racially and religiously between the immigrant Aryan groups and the older inhabitants, such as those belonging to the Dravidian people groups, which led to the further development of Hinduism.

The fact that the gospel of Jesus Christ was preached at least a thousand years ago (and probably two thousand) to the Hindus cannot be repudiated. Some of the present-day Christians in southern India are descendants of people who originally embraced the Good News. The contribution of Christians to Indian social, educational, political, and economic life is enormous: Many leaders of the freedom struggle came from the Christian community, and even now Christians in India contribute their best by fully participating in all spheres of life, working shoulder to shoulder with their Hindu and Muslim friends.

The British, who united India as a single political unit through accession of various sorts (and not always legally or uprightly), were ambivalent about the place of Christianity in India almost from the beginning of their rule. Preaching of the gospel was to be a private religious effort, not to be supported by the Crown. There were many incidents in which British officialdom took steps to curb missionary activities. So then, people came to Christ mainly through the voluntary work of the missionaries, not by any support of the ruling British monarchy.

There is no denying that the message of Christ is foreign to Hindu theology. Again, there are so many differences between the two that Hindus, instead of considering it simply foreign to their religion, look at it as a religion of foreigners. To me, theologically speaking, belief in Christ and belief in Hinduism are in conflict with one another (there *are* vast differences between the two), but Christianity is *not* a religion of foreigners: People of different nations, colors, and communities all over the world have embraced Jesus as their Lord and Savior, while remaining as nationalistic and patriotic as ever. In fact, the Word of God ordains submission to governmental authority, and Christians willingly follow the righteous laws of the lands in which they live.

Hindus are willing to embrace "foreign" technologies, become trained in "foreign" warfare, adopt "foreign" eating habits and other ways of life, and cross seas to accumulate wealth, without considering any of these things forbidden or illegal. But when it comes to religion, they consider anything other than Hinduism foreign, even though the church in India is at least a thousand years old, and about thirty million people in India profess to follow Christ.

There is a strange love/hate relationship between the secular social reformers who seek to modernize Hindu communities by doing away with traditions and those who believe in upholding tradition at any cost. Social reformers wish to replace religious practices with secular practices; at the same time, they also encourage a revival of interest in folk culture, religion, and the arts as a part of seeking, establishing, and fostering national, ethnic, and communal identities.

TRADITION DEFINED

Tradition is transmitting established beliefs, customs, ways, or methods from one generation to the next. Tradition is a strong source of strength and sustenance for Hindu religious practices; often tradition and nothing else is offered as the rationale. Tradition is respected, and the source of tradition is considered to be dependable, reliable, and full of wisdom. A traditional belief is not considered to be a novelty or invented, and no individual has the right to alter it. However, leaders *can* reinterpret it and establish new traditions within the parameters of original traditions. These may be transmitted orally, in writing, or both. Charismatic movements, dominant theology, or secular trends sometimes force change.

TRADITION AND REVIVALISM

Tradition is continuity, and modernization is beginning anew. The revival of folk arts and folk religion has become an integral part of nation building all over the world, especially in developing countries. The spiritual power or practice of folk religion may not be encouraged because these may come into conflict with the so-called scientific perspective that these nations want to inculcate in their citizens. However, governments extend support to folk culture and religious symbols that establish national identities.

Modern Hinduism gives up some traditions while it reiterates others, going back to practice what classical Sanskrit scriptures say has become common. The folk religious practices are greatly encouraged because the leaders see in them a source to increase the loyalty of the people toward their religion. Hinduism does not reject the folk counterpart of its scripture-based religion; it sees this as a legitimate part of Hinduism, satisfying the spiritual needs of the uninitiated and lower classes of people. Religious leaders criticize *only* those behaviors that are blatantly crude; there is a tussle between the gurus and the secular Hindus, because religious leaders always consider any attack on the practices of the folk Hindu religion as an attack on the main body of the religion. They may recognize the need for religious reformation, but they do not see any justification for giving up folk religion altogether.

TRADITION CAN ENSLAVE

Some well-known temples do not allow lower-caste people to enter and worship because tradition does not allow it; entry to caste-owned temples is restricted to that caste. People get involved in long, drawn-out legal battles in order to protect the traditions of their own sectarian groups, and worship routines for the idols must follow the tradition. Even a small change in the schedule, content, and form is a great cause for concern. Not following tradition leads not only to ritual pollution but is also seen as an insult to the elders and the memory of the dead.

Female feticide or infanticide is practiced by certain castes as tradition. Dedicating girls as temple dancers or as prostitutes is practiced in some parts even today because tradition sanctions it. Widow burning (*sati*, where widows of deceased husbands are burned alive), banned more than a century ago, keeps happening and is eulogized against the law. Hindus spend huge sums to celebrate the weddings of their children, borrowing money far beyond their means. The menace of the dowry is looming larger and larger, and hundreds of dowry-related suicides and killings are reported every year. The place of women in Hindu society and the education of Hindu girls leave much to be desired. Traditional practices hinder social, economic, and political progress, and yet the movement toward eradicating evil traditions is feeble and sporadic. Women are even denied inheritance.

For millions of Hindus, piercing, flagellation, and many other forms of self-inflicted torture are acceptable behavior because they have been handed down as religious tradition. These practices may have been condemned as superstitious or barbaric or uncivilized by some seers or sacred texts of their religion, and Hindus may even acknowledge the truthfulness of such statements, yet *they are unable to overcome such practices because of tradition.* As we have already seen, God detests tradition when people are misled by it. The prophets in the Old Testament and the ministry of Jesus Christ in the Gospels are strong testimony against tradition's deadly grip.

THE APOSTLE PAUL ON TRADITION

Paul uses the word for tradition in an interesting manner when it comes to following the teaching of the Word of God.

> Now I praise you because you remember me in everything, and hold firmly to the traditions, just as I delivered them to you. (1 Corinthians 11:2 NASB)
> So then, brethren, stand firm and hold to the traditions which you were taught, whether by word of mouth or by let-

ter from us. (2 Thessalonians 2:15 NASB)

Paul utilizes "tradition" (*paradosis*) in an approving manner here. However, the purpose was to constitute "a denial that what he [Paul] preached originated with himself, and a claim for its divine authority" (*The Expanded Vine's Expository Dictionary of New Testament Words*, 1160).

The commentators Jamieson, Fausset, and Brown say,

> When the canon [the collection of the books of the Bible] was complete, the infallibility of the living men was transferred to the written Word, now the sole unerring guide, interpreted by the Holy Spirit. Little else has come down to us by the most *ancient* and *universal* tradition save this, the all-sufficiency of Scripture for salvation. Therefore, by tradition, we are constrained to cast off all tradition not contained in, or not provable by, Scripture. (1221, emphasis mine)

NOT BY TRADITION, BUT BY THE HOLY SPIRIT

The Word of God is explicit in its teaching that we are not to be led by tradition but by His Spirit.

> At that time Jesus went on the Sabbath through the grainfields, and His disciples became hungry and began to pick the heads of grain and eat. But when the Pharisees saw it, they said to Him, "Behold, Your disciples do what is not lawful to do on a Sabbath." But He said to them, "Have you not read what David did, when he became hungry, he and his companions; how he entered the house of God, and they ate the consecrated bread, which was not lawful for him to eat, nor for those with him, but for the priests alone? Or have you not read in the Law, that on the Sabbath the priests in the temple break the Sabbath, and are innocent? But I say to you, that something greater than the temple is here. But if you had known what this means, 'I desire compassion, and not a sacrifice,' you would not have condemned the innocent. For the Son of Man is Lord of the Sabbath" (Matthew 12:1–8 NASB).

> Then some Pharisees and scribes came to Jesus from Jerusalem, saying, "Why do Your disciples transgress the tradition of the elders? For they do not wash their hands when they eat bread." And He answered and said to them, "And why do

you yourselves transgress the commandment of God for the sake of your tradition? For God said, 'Honor your father and mother,' and, 'He who speaks evil of father or mother, let him be put to death.' But you say, 'Whoever shall say to his father or mother, "Anything of mine you might have been helped by has been given to God," he is not to honor his father or his mother.' And thus you invalidated the word of God for the sake of your tradition. You hypocrites, rightly did Isaiah prophesy of you, saying, 'This people honors me with their lips, but their heart is far away from me. But in vain do they worship me, teaching as doctrines the precepts of men' " (Matthew 15:1–9 NASB).

See to it that no one takes you captive through philosophy and empty deception, according to the tradition of men, according to the elementary principles of the world, rather than according to Christ. (Colossians 2:8 NASB)

And if you address as Father the One who impartially judges according to each man's work, conduct yourselves in fear during the time of your stay upon earth; knowing that you were not redeemed with perishable things like silver or gold from your futile way of life inherited from your forefathers. (1 Peter 1:17–18 NASB)

As I urged you upon my departure for Macedonia, remain on at Ephesus, in order that you may instruct certain men not to teach strange doctrines, nor to pay attention to myths and endless genealogies, which give rise to mere speculation rather than furthering the administration of God which is by faith. (1 Timothy 1:3–4 NASB)

But the Spirit explicitly says that in later times some will fall away from the faith, paying attention to deceitful spirits and doctrines of demons, by means of the hypocrisy of liars seared in their own conscience. . . . In pointing out these things to the brethren, you will be a good servant of Christ Jesus, constantly nourished on the words of the faith and of the sound doctrine which you have been following. But have nothing to do with worldly fables fit only for old women. On the other hand, discipline yourself for the purpose of godliness. (1 Timothy 4:1–2, 6–7 NASB)

SCRIPTURE, JESUS, AND TRADITION

In most established religions other than Protestantism, the authoritative tradition is often considered to be equivalent to scripture. If there is an apparent conflict between scripture and tradition, the light shed by tradition will be taken as the final word on the matter.

Jesus assumed a prophetic mold when He spoke against tradition, His intent being to restore the original intent of the Father in the spiritual and material life of humankind. He used several expressions such as "It is written" and "You have heard that it was said to the men of old." These sayings showed His audience that He was standing within the tradition, and what He preached was what the tradition really meant. He declared that He did not come to negate the law, but to fulfill it; in the fulfilling of the intent of the law, Jesus, indeed, changed and abrogated the law as seen and practiced by tradition. This is why a conflict started between the interpretation of the written law on the one hand and a living Master on the other. Jesus showed the Pharisees that they actually left the commandments of God and held fast to the traditions of men (Mark 7:8; Matthew 15:1–9).

Consider Matthew 5:21–22: "You have heard that it was said to the people long ago, 'Do not murder, and anyone who murders will be subject to judgment.' But I tell you that anyone who is angry with his brother will be subject to judgment."

Jesus was changing the understanding of the law in a revolutionary way. In this process He often cited the traditional authorities to illumine and support what He declared: "He replied, 'Isaiah was right when he prophesied about you hypocrites; as it is written: "These people honor me with their lips, but their hearts are far from me. They worship me in vain; their teachings are but rules taught by men" ' " (Mark 7:6–7).

Hinduism provides for every taste and every inclination, recognizing that there may be many ways to reach and be in union with the Supreme Being. One may be intellectually oriented and choose the path of knowledge to realize his union with the divine; or, he may be inclined toward a personal devotion to the divine, worshiping through rituals and other performing acts; or, he may be inclined to do works through dutiful rituals and action to be in position to have communion with the divine.

WHAT IS SUPERSTITION?

Hindu social and religious reformers have attacked the beliefs and practices of Hindus that they consider superstitious; these have sought to educate their people on grounds that these beliefs and practices are based on ignorance and fear of the unknown and are not substantiated by actual facts. Often they have taken the position that if scientific temper is inculcated among Hindus, superstition will decrease or be totally eliminated—spread of literacy will change the outlook regarding superstitious practices.

But this is not happening. Many Hindus see that people in distant countries emulate their "superstitious" beliefs and practices. For example, they observe that astrology is popular in Western countries. They read in the newspapers that various occult practices are reported through "scientific" experiments to be beneficial. A sense of pride develops in the minds of people when they see that their beliefs and practices are accepted, and this leads to confirmation of the correctness, if not superiority, of their own beliefs. This further encourages superstition.

The current meaning of the word *superstition* emphasizes that an act is superstitious if it cannot be explained or understood with reason; when a cause-and-effect relationship cannot be established for a belief, it will be considered superstitious. But this is an inadequate understanding of religious practices, and it leads to a description of many religious beliefs as superstition. *The greatest of all superstitions is the unproven "scientific" belief that if something cannot be explained through empirical proof, then it should be considered superstitious.* Religious experience often *is* beyond reason and lies in the realm of faith and subjective experience. If this position is accepted, the religious beliefs of Hindus cannot be completely and unilaterally rejected as superstition. However, even Hindus own up to the fact that certain practices breed fear and lead to enslavement.

HOW DOES THE WORD OF GOD VIEW SUPERSTITION?

The Greek word used for superstition (*desidaimonia*) refers to the fear of the gods or fear of pagan deity and is used "with a condemnatory or contemptuous significance" (*The Expanded Vine's Expository Dictionary of New Testament Words*, 944). Festus used this word to refer to Judaism in Acts 25:19; in Acts 17:22 it is used in the sense of being excessively religious.

The following instances recorded in the Bible illustrate instances of superstition:

(1) the Israelites' supposing that their defeat in battle with the Philistines was due to their not having brought with them the ark of the covenant (1 Samuel 4:3; 10–11);

(2) the Philistines' refusing to tread the threshold of the temple of Dagon after the image of Dagon had repeatedly fallen (1 Samuel 5:5);

(3) the belief of the Syrians concerning the help of the gods (1 Kings 20:23);

(4) the Jews' attributing their calamities to having ceased offering sacrifices to the Queen of Heaven (Jeremiah 44:17–19);

(5) Nebuchadnezzar's supposing that the spirit of the gods was upon Daniel (Daniel 4:8–9);

(6) the sailors' casting Jonah into the sea (Jonah 1:4–16);

(7) the disciples' supposing they saw a spirit when Jesus came to them walking on the water (Matthew 14:26; Mark 6:49–50);

(8) Herod's imagining that John the Baptist had risen from the dead (Mark 6:14, 16);

(9) the Gadarenes' reacting to Jesus casting devils out of the possessed man (Matthew 8:34);

(10) the disciples' being frightened at the appearance of Peter (Acts 12:14–15);

(11) the Ephesians' indulging in their sorceries (Acts 19:13–19);

(12) the people of the island of Malta imagining Paul to be a god (Acts 28:6). (Nave, 980–81)

According to the Word of God, an act, belief, or worship that draws from forces outside of God is superstition and is not acceptable to Him—He is even portrayed as being impatient and angry with those who followed superstition. However, in His anger is the solace that it is directed against those who seek superstition only because it pollutes them. Remember Leviticus 19:31: "Do not turn to mediums or seek out spiritists, for you will be defiled by them. I am the LORD your God." From a theological perspective, the consequence that superstition brings upon its practitioners is terrible.

SUPERSTITION BRINGS FEAR AND UNCERTAINTY

Superstition produces dread and unsteadiness. On the other hand, fear of God is love of God, and fear of God turns into love, prosperity, and blessing. Superstition brings fear because the inherent character-istic of superstition is its uncertainty. *This* fear (of uncertainty) brings bondage, while the fear of God brings freedom, because God is the source of all assurance and certainty. He is unchanging and constant.

> The LORD Almighty is the one you are to regard as holy, he is the one you are to fear, he is the one you are to dread, and he will be a sanctuary. . . . When men tell you to consult mediums and spiritists, who whisper and mutter, should not a people inquire of their God? Why consult the dead on behalf of the living? To the law and to the testimony! If they do not speak according to this word, they have no light of dawn. (Isaiah 8:13–14, 19–20)

Superstition does not deliver what it promises:

> So do not listen to your prophets, your diviners, your interpreters of dreams, your mediums or your sorcerers who tell you, "You will not serve the king of Babylon." They prophesy lies to you that will only serve to remove you far from your lands. (Jeremiah 27:9)

As Daniel declared, "No wise man, enchanter, magician or diviner can explain to the king the mystery he has asked about, but there is a God in heaven who reveals mysteries" (2:27–28).

THE PLACE OF SUPERSTITION IN HINDUISM

Superstition is a theological problem within Christianity, but for the Hindus in general, and for the Hindu social reformers in particular, it is merely a socioeconomic and literacy issue; because they cannot confront it within their theology—since their theology tolerates superstitious acts—their attempt to eradicate the social, economic, and other consequences of superstition is bound to fail. In their case, successful eradication of superstition would mean the loss of their religion.

In religious groups, people commonly tend to resort to superstition in relation to birth, love, sickness, and death, wherein humans experience greater anxiety—which is indeed a trap. We as Christians need to encourage our Hindu friends to focus on the assurance of the Lord Jesus Christ, who is always with us. One of the reasons for belief in and practice of superstition among Hindus is the firm belief that fate cannot be overcome. *Fatalism encourages superstition*, and people develop superstitious acts to reduce the severity of the consequence of fate or even to escape from it. However, the saving grace of Jesus cleanses us from all our sins and transforms us; fate has no hold over us once we accept Him as Lord and Savior. This good news has liberated millions of people all over the world from their slavery to superstition, leading them to joy. This point, when explained to our Hindu neighbors in a manner that shows our love for them and our concern for their life (*never* in a condemnatory tone or with an air of superiority), will glow in their hearts. Their fear of fate and dependence upon superstition can lose its hold over them!

IDOL WORSHIP

13

In Hinduism (as well as Shinto and Buddhism), idol or image worship plays a prominent and approved role within the scriptural or high religion. The word *idol* is derived from the Greek *eidolon*, meaning a likeness to the object it represents. An idol, for this purpose, is a similitude of a supposed deity or divinity used for worship.

There is also another word, *icon*, which should be considered here. This comes from the Greek *eikon*, which means an image, figure, representation, or portrait, and it usually refers to such objects of worship that are more easily transportable than idols. *Iconography* refers to the art of representing, or making visible, the religious or legendary subjects.

Idolatry is a combination of two Greek words: the aforementioned *eidolon* ("image") and also *latreia* ("adoration"). Idolatry, then, is the adoration of objects, the expression of dependence, especially through sacrifice and rituals. Idolatry is the worship of what is considered to be a substitute for the divine, and Hinduism represents the most widely prevalent and intricate system of idol worship.

Idolatry is closely related to, springs from, and supports polytheism (belief in more than one god) and animism (worship of spiritual beings). Animism helps the perception that idols are the abode of spiritual beings; in polytheistic societies, iconography, the art of carving or making idols, is highly valued art in the religious sense. However, most Hebrew (biblical) words denoting idols and idolatry are inherently pejorative and contemptuous, referring to vanity, nothingness, or even excrement.

IDOLATRY—A MISGUIDED HUMAN EFFORT

Iconography—allegedly, gods made visible—is a misdirected attempt on the part of man to establish a personal relationship with God. Originally, people did walk with God, hearing His voice, listening to Him, and calling upon Him.

> When Enoch had lived 65 years, he became the father of Methuselah. And after he became the father of Methuselah, Enoch walked with God 300 years and had other sons and daughters. Altogether, Enoch lived 365 years. Enoch walked with God; then he was no more, because God took him away. (Genesis 5:21–24)

In idol worship, direct contact with God is exchanged in favor of direct contact with an image supposed to be a god. This is clearly illustrated by the Israelites in the wilderness. Their leader, Moses, was not readily available to lead and counsel them because he had gone to the mountain to take care of business with God; in desperation, they took things into their own hands:

> When the people saw that Moses was so long in coming down from the mountain, they gathered around Aaron and said, "Come, make us gods who will go before us. As for this fellow Moses who brought us up out of Egypt, we don't know what has happened to him." Aaron answered them, "Take off the gold earrings that your wives, your sons and your daughters are wearing, and bring them to me." So all the people took off their earrings and brought them to Aaron. He took what they handed him and made it into an idol cast in the shape of a calf, fashioning it with a tool. Then they said, "These are your gods, O Israel, who brought you up out of Egypt" (Exodus 32:1–4).

This early picture of idol-making also shows the earthly side of this seemingly spiritual experience:

> When Aaron saw this, he built an altar in front of the calf and announced, "Tomorrow there will be a festival to the LORD." So the next day the people rose early and sacrificed burnt offerings and presented fellowship offerings. Afterward they sat down to eat and drink and got up to indulge in revelry. (Exodus 32:5–6)

IDOLATRY—HUMANS PLAYING GOD

Idol-making as a religious pursuit is also a reversal of what God did by creating humankind in His image: humanity, in response, attempts to make gods in its own image. God created animate beings, whereas an idol-maker creates inanimate objects.

Man's view of God is often desperately skewed—even among the Israelites a representation of deity was manifested as an animal (a calf). Polytheistic/pantheistic societies do not necessarily represent their spiritual beings or Supreme Being in human form; often they admire the strength of such things as animals, and they represent their gods with unusual human features or in animal form to show their alleged power. Idol worshipers may treat their trade tools as gods, worshiping and offering sacrifices to them. However, the Word of God condemns every type of idol worship:

> The wicked foe pulls all of them up with hooks, he catches them in his net, he gathers them up in his dragnet; and so he rejoices and is glad. Therefore he sacrifices to his net and burns incense to his dragnet, for by his net he lives in luxury and enjoys the choicest food. Is he to keep on emptying his net, destroying nations without mercy? (Habakkuk 1:15–17)

Every human being is given general revelation about God:

> What may be known about God is plain to them, because God has made it plain to them. For since the creation of the world God's invisible qualities—his eternal power and divine nature—have been clearly seen, being understood from what has been made, so that men are without excuse. For although they knew God, they neither glorified him as God nor gave thanks to him, but their thinking became futile and their foolish hearts were darkened. Although they claimed to be wise, they became fools and exchanged the glory of the immortal God for images made to look like mortal man and birds and animals and reptiles. (Romans 1:19–23; see also Ecclesiastes 3:11)

How do we communicate the message of the Word of God to Hindus without showing condemnation or an air of superiority? Doing so can be especially hard because Hindus see the zeal with which the Roman Catholic Church venerates images, and they wonder why another section of Christians should be so adamantly against image worship.

SANCTITY AND INNOVATIONS

There is no limit to the imagination and practice of idol-making among Hindus—they may use sand, stone, clay, leaves, hides, wood, metal, chalk, glass, or cloth. They may represent dead persons, childhood stages, body parts, geometric figures, or animals. However, established traditions do limit freedom by sanctioning only those forms that have been approved in the oral or written traditions. Innovations are often resented.

Idols function as mediating objects to an underlying belief system, and if the link between the two is weak, idol worship is likely to be weakened. This connection (between image worship and the belief system) *was* broken in the Greek and Roman worlds when the gospel was preached; as a consequence, idol worship is now a rare phenomenon in the West, even among the nations in which many do not follow Christian theology. Idols have become instead objects of art in these areas.

On the other hand, among Hindus, the link between their belief system and idol worship is very strong, and idol worship continues to be the chief form of religious expression.

JUSTIFICATION FOR IDOL WORSHIP

Some of the justifications for image worship offered within Hindu thought are as follows. (Several are similar to those offered by the Eastern Orthodox Church to support their deep veneration of icons, and others resemble those offered by the Roman Catholic Church.)

(1) Idols are not mere toys; they are centers of high psychic power and energy.
(2) Gazing at an image of god awakens man's subconscious mind, and if he can respond to the powerful magnetism of the deity, he is able to realize the grandeur of the Paramaatman (the Universal Soul) through the medium of the image into which his concentration penetrates.
(3) Images have been used only to illustrate concepts.
(4) Sculptors are not satisfied with realistic portrayal. They create the images in a manner that would instigate higher thinking in humans.

(5) Images are created with exaggerated shapes and body parts in order to create in laypeople a sense of special feeling, extraordinary wonderment, and devotion.

(6) Images are made big and beautiful to demonstrate to ordinary people that divine beings have much greater power than human beings.

(7) Images of the gods are meant to be symbols that reveal the hidden, original, and real truth. They are created to indicate the philosophy or theology that lies within and beyond the images themselves.

(8) An image has to be understood as a symbol meant to keep before the eye of the worshiper certain attributes of the deity he undertakes to worship and upon which he desires to concentrate his thoughts. (Srinivasan, 117–130)

ENCOURAGEMENT FOR IDOLATRY

The intercessory roles assigned to the saints (and such personages whose images are objects of veneration) encourage idol worship. The attitude toward and the acceptance of the iconographic representation of Christian personages and events and treating them as objects of veneration, if not worship, has become one of the dividing chasms between the Catholic and Protestant faiths.

The Reformers assigned an intellectual function to the use of iconography in the church. For them, the representation was to focus upon religious thought and theological propositions rather than emphasis on meditation and prayer with the help of icons, as is done in Hinduism. On the other hand, the emphasis in the Roman Catholic and Eastern Orthodox Churches was on the role and function of the images and icons in the spiritual life of the faithful.

Idol worship entered the church through the traditions brought in by newly converted pagans. Although there was stiff opposition to image worship of the pagan gods, opposition to the veneration of Christian images was not unanimous, mainly because of the influence of pagan culture and polity. We can easily trace the process of the increase in popularity of image worship in church history as a consequence of growing dependence on tradition. Those who steadfastly opposed image worship were soon branded as heretics.

A growing number of church leaders and theologians began to justify image worship over the centuries. For a brief interlude, image worship was even banned by rulers, soon to be reestablished with great vigor and vengeance. Image worship and attendant veneration of Mary and of the saints and their relics became the cornerstone of the theology and piety of the Roman Catholic Church. The Word of God took a backseat until the Reformation.

How Do They Make the Idols Look Alive?

Since idols by themselves are immobile, Hindus have rituals, festivals, and other observances to bring mobility to them. This is carried out in several ways: People may worship an animate object, such as a cow or a snake, in place of the idols; they may take the idols in procession around the town with accompanying music, assuming that the gods are visiting the mortals; they may create stories to portray the idols to be mobile and powerful; they may attach cosmic symbols like the halo or arch around the idols. Some gods are made into idols with certain postures of mobility, such as a lifted leg, an extended hand or palm for blessing, a bowed head, a smile, a displaced ornament, some object underfoot, a particular posture that shows activity, extension of the tongue, or plurality of faces or other body parts.

The Bible on Idol Worship

The Word of God condemns idol or image worship in any form; following are some passages of Scripture that address the issue:

> Why do the nations say, "Where is their God?" Our God is in heaven; he does whatever pleases him. But their idols are silver and gold, made by the hands of men. They have mouths, but cannot speak, eyes, but they cannot see; they have ears, but cannot hear, noses, but they cannot smell; they have hands, but cannot feel, feet, but they cannot walk; nor can they utter a sound with their throats. Those who make them will be like them, and so will all who trust in them. (Psalm 115:2–8)

> Half of the wood he burns in the fire; over it he prepares his meal, he roasts his meat and eats his fill. He also warms himself and says, "Ah! I am warm; I see the fire." From the rest he makes a god, his idol; he bows down to it and worships. He prays to it and says, "Save me; you are my god." They know nothing, they understand nothing; their eyes are

plastered over so they cannot see, and their minds closed so they cannot understand. No one stops to think, no one has the knowledge or understanding to say, "Half of it I used for fuel; I even baked bread over its coals, I roasted meat and I ate. Shall I make a detestable thing from what is left? Shall I bow down to a block of wood?" He feeds on ashes, a deluded heart misleads him; he cannot save himself, or say, "Is not this thing in my right hand a lie?" (Isaiah 44:16–20).

You shall not make for yourself an idol in the form of anything in heaven above or on the earth beneath or in the waters below. You shall not bow down to them or worship them; for I, the LORD your God, am a jealous God. (Exodus 20:4–5)

Cursed is the man who carves an image or casts an idol— a thing detestable to the LORD, the work of the craftsman's hands—and sets it up in secret. (Deuteronomy 27:15)

The Spirit lifted me up between earth and heaven and in visions of God he took me to Jerusalem, to the entrance to the north gate of the inner court, where the idol that provokes to jealousy stood. . . . I saw this idol of jealousy. . . . [Then] he said to me, "Son of man, do you see what they are doing— the utterly detestable things the house of Israel is doing here, things that will drive me far from my sanctuary?" (Ezekiel 8:3–6).

They consult a wooden idol and are answered by a stick of wood. A spirit of prostitution leads them astray; they are unfaithful to their God. (Hosea 4:12)

Of what value is an idol, since a man has carved it? Or an image that teaches lies? For he who makes it trusts in his own creation; he makes idols that cannot speak. Woe to him who says to wood, "Come to life!" Or to lifeless stone, "Wake up!" Can it give guidance? It is covered with gold and silver; there is no breath in it. But the LORD is in his holy temple; let all the earth be silent before him. (Habakkuk 2:18–19)

For rebellion is like the sin of divination, and arrogance like the evil of idolatry. (1 Samuel 15:23)

But they would not listen and were as stiff-necked as their fathers, who did not trust in the LORD their God. They rejected his decrees and the covenant he had made with their fathers and the warnings he had given them. They followed worthless idols and themselves became worthless. (2 Kings 17:14–15)

For all the gods of the nations are idols, but the LORD

made the heavens. (1 Chronicles 16:26)

Son of man, these men have set up idols in their hearts and put wicked stumbling blocks before their faces. Should I let them inquire of me at all? Therefore speak to them and tell them, "This is what the Sovereign LORD says: 'When any Israelite sets up idols in his heart and puts a wicked stumbling block before his face and then goes to a prophet, I the LORD will answer him myself in keeping with his great idolatry. I will do this to recapture the hearts of the people of Israel, who have all deserted me for their idols.' Therefore say to the house of Israel, 'This is what the Sovereign LORD says: Repent! Turn from your idols and renounce all your detestable practices!' " (Ezekiel 14:3–6).

The idols speak deceit, diviners see visions that lie; they tell dreams that are false, they give comfort in vain. Therefore the people wander like sheep oppressed for lack of a shepherd. (Zechariah 10:2)

At Horeb they made a calf and worshiped an idol cast from metal. They exchanged their Glory for an image of a bull, which eats grass. (Psalm 106:19–20)

So then, about eating food sacrificed to idols: We know that an idol is nothing at all in the world and that there is no God but one. For even if there are so-called gods, whether in heaven or on earth (as indeed there are many "gods" and many "lords"), yet for us there is but one God, the Father, from whom all things came and for whom we live; and there is but one Lord, Jesus Christ, through whom all things came and through whom we live. (1 Corinthians 8:4–6)

Do I mean then that a sacrifice offered to an idol is anything, or that an idol is anything? No, but the sacrifices of pagans are offered to demons, not to God, and I do not want you to be participants with demons. You cannot drink the cup of the Lord and the cup of demons too; you cannot have a part in both the Lord's table and the table of demons. Are we trying to arouse the Lord's jealousy? Are we stronger than he? (1 Corinthians 10:19–22)

But now I am writing you that you must not associate with anyone who calls himself a brother but is sexually immoral or greedy, an idolater or a slanderer, a drunkard or a swindler. With such a man do not even eat. (1 Corinthians 5:11)

For of this you can be sure: No immoral, impure or greedy person—such a man is an idolater—has any inheritance in the kingdom of Christ and of God. (Ephesians 5:5)

Do not be idolaters, as some of them were; as it is written: "The people sat down to eat and drink and got up to indulge in pagan revelry" (1 Corinthians 10:7).

But the cowardly, the unbelieving, the vile, the murderers, the sexually immoral, those who practice magic arts, the idolaters and all liars—their place will be in the fiery lake of burning sulfur. This is the second death. (Revelation 21:8)

The acts of the sinful nature are obvious: sexual immorality, impurity and debauchery; idolatry and witchcraft; hatred, discord, jealousy, fits of rage, selfish ambition, dissensions, factions and envy; drunkenness, orgies, and the like. I warn you, as I did before, that those who live like this will not inherit the kingdom of God. (Galatians 5:19–21)

Put to death, therefore, whatever belongs to your earthly nature: sexual immorality, impurity, lust, evil desires and greed, which is idolatry. (Colossians 3:5)

It is my judgment, therefore, that we should not make it difficult for the Gentiles who are turning to God. Instead we should write to them, telling them to abstain from food polluted by idols, from sexual immorality, from the meat of strangled animals and from blood. (Acts 15:19–20)

Dear children, keep yourselves from idols. (1 John 5:21)

The god of this age has blinded the minds of unbelievers, so that they cannot see the light of the gospel of the glory of Christ, who is the image of God. (2 Corinthians 4:4)

He is the image of the invisible God, the firstborn over all creation. For by him all things were created: things in heaven and on earth, visible and invisible, whether thrones or powers or rulers or authorities; all things were created by him and for him. (Colossians 1:15–16)

Remember, the Word of God says that the battle against idol worship will continue until the very end of this world. Such is the force of deception that many will not change even after great plagues:

The rest of mankind that were not killed by these plagues still did not repent of the work of their hands; they did not stop worshiping demons, and idols of gold, silver, bronze, stone and wood—idols that cannot see or hear or walk. Nor did they repent of their murders, their magic arts, their sexual immorality or their thefts. (Revelation 9:20–21)

VARIOUS KINDS OF IDOL WORSHIP

It is obvious from the above verses that idol worship practiced in any form is against God. But those given to image worship actually think that through it they are getting closer to their gods or goddesses. There is often a *strong* emotional attachment to certain images. Only when they accept Jesus Christ will our Hindu friends begin to see the reasons why God detests image worship.

You can show how idols are treated like favor-disbursing vending machines. Since the thief as well as the noble man seeks the help of the very same idol for the success of his efforts, it's obvious that image worship does not inculcate in the worshiper any higher ideals or sanctify him as a fit vessel of God. The myths and characteristics attributed to the images are far from perfect, and this can become an interesting subject for conversation if raised with caution, love, and understanding. You will be able to reach these conclusions directly from your Hindu friend if you allow him to speak on his own without interruption. At the right moment, you may cite a verse or two to show how God wants us to worship Him in holiness and not depend on material objects. Tell him that God is at hand to help us.

If your friend makes a point of performing rituals (*puja*) before the pictures or images of gods and goddesses on a daily basis, you can help wean him away from this practice by fervent prayer, seeking a revelation in his heart and soul. A ritual Hindu would need something miraculous in his life to understand the glory of God. Pray that his personal needs are met through the prayers you offer on his behalf. The best course is to pray (in his presence) for his special needs and trust that the Lord will answer your prayers in a fashion that demonstrates a link between your prayer and the fulfillment of his needs.

Idol worship is not only the worship of carved images. *Any act or object that takes our focus away from the Lord and to itself is an idol*, which is detestable to God. Creating wealth or striving hard to build and improve one's career is justifiable, but if all our focus is only on such matters, and if we seek gratification or fulfillment for our lives only through such things, our career, our wealth, and our family will all take the form and function of idol worship.

HOW DO WE DEAL WITH IDOLATROUS CULTURES?

You must realize that removing image worship from an idolatrous culture, even after the acceptance of the gospel of Jesus Christ, will prove to be a tremendous challenge. In the name of preservation of the heritage, culture-lovers and culture-mongers tend to retain the elements of idol-worship as objects of art. Violent demonstration of the powerlessness of idols by treading them underfoot, or breaking or mutilating them, will not solve the problem but will only add to the confusion and hatred between the Christian and the non-Christian. Often the new Christian is not convinced of the need to throw out these objects, because they have given him comfort and direction in his past spiritual life. It was quite exasperating even to the early church fathers to lead the newly converted away from idol worship. For example, Augustine (354–430), in his *Sermons on New Testament Lessons* (Sermon 12), suggests the following (Schaff, 303):

> Many pagans have these abominations on their own estates; do we go and break them in pieces? No, for our first efforts are that the idols in their hearts should be broken down. When they too are made Christians themselves, they either invite us to so good a work, or anticipate us. At present we must pray for them, not be angry with them. If very painful feelings excite us, it is rather against Christians, it is against our brethren, who will enter into the Church in such a mind, as to have their body there, and their heart anywhere else.

Continuous preaching from the Word of God in the churches, constant vigil kept by the new believers about their own acts of commission and omission, and continuing prayers against falling back into the habit of image worship will help us.

GODS AND GODDESSES

14

Some religions, such as Hinduism, abound in gods and goddesses, and this is not considered objectionable. Sometimes where the people profess to worship only one god or God, gods and goddesses are still accommodated under folk religious practices. Where there is a multiplicity of gods, one god is elevated to the highest level (henotheism), and others become helpers and assistants or co-equal to the highest god. The elements or characteristics of the high god may be magnified and assumed to be the basis for the creation and worship of additional gods. Gods and goddesses in this scheme become the representation of the characteristics of some divine reality.

Among Hindus, there is a general sense of a Supreme Being, but this Supreme Being manifests himself in the form of gods and goddesses. There is no single God who is considered to be the Supreme Being; it all depends upon the sect to which a Hindu belongs. If your friend hails from a sect/family that worships Vishnu, he may consider Vishnu to be the Supreme Being. If your friend comes from a sect/family that worships Shiva, he may consider Shiva to be the Supreme Being. If your friend belongs to a sect/family that worships Kali or Sakti (a goddess), he may consider Kali or Sakti to be the Supreme Being.

Sectarian feelings may be very strong in some households or communities, but this does not really reflect the practices of Hinduism. The avatar (roughly translated as "incarnation") principle links one manifestation of a god to his other manifestations and establishes a network of gods and goddesses, all belonging to a pantheon. Each god or goddess has a function to perform, and more often than not, gods and goddesses have their own attributes.

CULTURE TYPES AND GODS

Anthropologists often tend to classify gods and goddesses based on the type of society. For example, it is suggested that the hunter-and-food-gatherer societies create gods from culture heroes in animal form, which function as masters and mistresses of animals. There is thus a close association between the type of society and the kinds of gods and goddesses that are created and worshiped.

The planting cultures have earth gods of fertility along with animal gods. In these cultures, culture heroes are those who discovered or invented the cultivated plants; for example, the Hindus believe that Indra brought sugarcane to the chief of gods and goddesses. Planting cultures also abound in atmospheric gods such as storm, thunder, rain, and sun.

In the pastoral societies, herds of animals, along with atmospheric gods, are honored. The herds of animals have divine powers.

In societies where there is a clear division of labor, we find pantheons of gods, closely resembling and modeling the social hierarchy found in the human society. Such is the case among Hindus.

All these go to show that gods and goddesses are the product of humans and that their hierarchy and characteristics may be modeled after human characteristics and the hierarchy of the society. Gods and goddesses reflect the value system of a society.

PANTHEON

The term *pantheon* refers to all the gods of a people. Hindu gods are well organized in terms of a hierarchy; each god or goddess has a function and form.

In the Hindu pantheon, gods and goddesses are marked for their relative status to one another—they may form their own kinship groups; they may be distinguished in terms of their avocation; they may marry one another; they may beget their own children. They may fight among themselves to establish their own territory or supremacy; they may be jealous of one another; they may make war and peace and take sides with humans; they may participate in the lives of their devotees; they may take several avatars and come down to earth to live and act like humans. The activities of gods and goddesses are all mythological, not historical. Yet the devotees may see no distinction between the two, for, after all, the gods descend and take possession of humans and speak through them to their devotees.

A special feature of the Hindu pantheon is that if a god or goddess has some worth he or she will have his or her own personal animal transportation and abode. For example, Shiva and his wife supposedly live on one of the peaks of the Himalayas, called Kailash. Vishnu has his own upper-world abode called the Vaikunth. Shiva's personal mode of transportation is a bull, whereas Vishnu's personal mode of transportation, in one of his several avatars, is a *garuda* (eagle). Even these personal animals may be worshiped as gods, and sometimes they perform the function of mediator between the deity and the devotee.

Some of the gods may indulge in polygamous relationships; some may remain unmarried and eternally young; they all drink elixir-like nectar, available only to them; some may covet the wives of other deities. There is no end to their *leela* (sport).

GODS OF ELITIST AND FOLK RELIGIONS

The deities of the Hindu pantheon reflect the social values or status of the worshipers; for example, the gods and goddesses worshiped by high-caste Hindus are mostly vegetarian, and they are often shown to be light-skinned; the gods and goddesses of other castes are often dark-skinned.

The gods and goddesses of higher castes also occupy the higher positions in the pantheon, and those of the lower castes are relegated to lower strata. The gods and goddesses of the lower castes often descend and occupy the bodies of their worshipers who fall into a trance as a sign of such occupation, whereas the gods and goddesses of higher castes generally do not enter into the bodies of their worshipers or make them fall into a trance.

The gods and goddesses of upper castes are often worshiped with recitation of verses from the Sanskrit language, the language of the Hindu scriptures. Those of the lower castes are worshiped with the recitation of verses from the vernacular. Many more differences may be cited, all of which coincide with the characteristics often adduced as a sign of social status.

Another type of god consists of the earth deities. The earth is often portrayed to be Mother; Bhumaadevi, goddess of the earth, is popular among Hindus. Mountains, rivers, water, trees, plants, and ocean are all part of the earth gods and goddesses.

Yet another type consists of those coming from the underworld. Animistic religions and folk religious parts of the monotheistic religions abound in descriptions of the underworld powers, usually dreaded and avoided. Yet humans cannot escape from being subjected to torture or scrutiny by these powers in their passage from the realm of the living to the realm of the dead. Yama is a god of death; he rides a black buffalo and has a long robe to catch the unwilling dying person to take him to the abode he deserves.

There are also gods and goddesses who perform earthly social functions; their domain of operation directly relates to the social life and hierarchy of humans. Many of these gods and goddesses focus on fertility and prosperity, while some focus their operation on the means of acquisition and use of physical power and bravery. There are gods and goddesses who are seen to be the creators and guardians of society and order. There are others of healing, sickness, and death.

There are also gods of culture. For example, knowledge and arts, including fine arts and aesthetics, are the provenance of Saraswati. Hindus worship her by taking a day off from study. There is likewise a special day of celebration for the god of technology during which all the implements will be washed and oiled with great care and devotion. Because theirs is an idol-worshiping culture, Hindus have elevated even the languages they speak to the status of goddesses. Images are set up to represent the goddess of specific languages and these are offered praise and worship. There are also gods of magic and gods of secret arts.

GODS ARE PERSONAL SPIRITUAL BEINGS

Remember that gods and goddesses are personal spiritual beings—they have their own names; they have their own cosmic and social functions; they have their own abodes; they may be presented in the form of distinct images and worshiped. They even have their own family relationships and functions both within the cosmic society of gods and the earthly society of humans. Usually elaborate rituals of worship may be offered to them depending upon the perception of their value by the human worshipers. They may be forgotten and thrown away as "useless divinity," or they may be highly cherished. A god who was popular in one generation may not be even recognized in another generation. A god who occupied the central place of worship in the sanctum sanctorum of a temple may be downgraded, and the community may not even offer infrequent prayers to him. A god who may have been greatly loved and admired may be despised and avoided in another era.

THE TRUTH BEHIND GODS

While it is true that the vast majority of gods and goddesses are given *forms* by humans, the *existence* of gods and goddesses as personal spiritual beings cannot be denied. Humans who created the forms of gods and goddesses knew there was some basis behind what they were doing. Spiritual beings all around us are worshiped in the Hindu religion without any reservation. How do we communicate the truth to our Hindu neighbors?

The Word of God declares: "Fear the LORD your God, serve him only and take your oaths in his name. Do not follow other gods, the gods of the peoples around you" (Deuteronomy 6:13–14).

God Most High, God Almighty, the LORD the Eternal, I AM THAT I AM, is so holy that humans were forbidden to see Him face to face or behold His glory (Genesis 32:30; Exodus 3:5), even though He said that He would be with us (Exodus 3:12). The Bible clearly says that our God does not want us to worship any other spiritual being (Exodus 34:14); God even made it very personal when He declared that He is a jealous God (Exodus 20:5). We are called upon not to misuse the name of the LORD our God (Exodus 20:7) or blaspheme or profane His name (Exodus 22:28; Leviticus 18:21).

God has ordered: "Do not make any gods to be alongside me; do not make for yourselves gods of silver or gods of gold" (Exodus 20:23)—"whoever sacrifices to any god other than the LORD must be destroyed" (Exodus 22:20). We are required to be holy because God is holy (Leviticus 21:6); He has promised to walk among us and be our God (Leviticus 26:12).

Our God is the God of the spirits of all humankind (Numbers 16:22; 27:16). Everything is subject to His sovereignty. Since God is not a man, He does not lie (Numbers 23:19). Judgment belongs to God (Deuteronomy 1:17); however, He is merciful (Deuteronomy

4:31). The LORD God is in heaven (Deuteronomy 4:39), but even the highest heavens cannot contain Him (2 Chronicles 2:6).

We should love the LORD our God with all our heart and with all our soul and with all our strength (Deuteronomy 6:5). We should fear the LORD our God, serve him only, and take our oaths in His name. We should not follow other gods, the gods of the peoples around us (Deuteronomy 6:13–14).

We should not test the LORD our God (Deuteronomy 6:16) except in finding out for ourselves the result of our tithes and offerings: "Test me in this," says the LORD Almighty, "and see if I will not . . . pour out so much blessing that you will not have room enough for it" (Malachi 3:10). We should understand that our God is the faithful God (Deuteronomy 7:19), that the LORD our God will keep his covenant (Deuteronomy 7:12), that He is a great and awesome God (Deuteronomy 7:21) and that He will discipline us (Deuteronomy 8:5).

The LORD our God is the God of gods (Deuteronomy 10:17), detesting anyone who deals dishonestly (Deuteronomy 25:16). The LORD our God also recognizes that the circumcision of the heart is more crucial and important than physical circumcision: "The LORD your God will circumcise your hearts, and the hearts of your descendants, so that you may love him with all your heart and with all your soul, and live" (Deuteronomy 30:6).

Our God is the faithful God who does no wrong, upright and just is He (Deuteronomy 32:4). And the eternal God is our refuge (Deuteronomy 33:27) who has declared: "See now that I myself am He! There is no god besides me. I put to death and I bring to life, I have wounded and I will heal, and no one can deliver out of my hand" (Deuteronomy 32:39).

Our God is not only the God of the hills; He is the God of the valleys also (1 Kings 20:28).

The Word of God refers to several gods of the nations by their names, thus recognizing the existence of other powers. But at the same time, it declares that our God is greater than all other gods (2 Chronicles 2:5). There is no god like Him in heaven or on earth (2 Chronicles 6:14).

Jesus said that no one is good except God alone (Mark 10:18; Luke 18:19). The right to become children of God is given to all who believe in Jesus' name and who receive Him as Lord and Savior (John

1:12). No one has ever seen God, but God the One and Only, who is at the Father's side, has made Him known to us through Jesus (John 1:18).

> Since we are God's offspring, we should not think that the divine being is like gold or silver or stone—an image made by man's design and skill. In the past God overlooked such ignorance, but now he commands all people everywhere to repent. (Acts 17:29–30)

> But now a righteousness from God, apart from law, has been made known, to which the Law and the Prophets testify. This righteousness from God comes through faith in Jesus Christ to all who believe. (Romans 3:21–22)

> Is God the God of Jews only? Is he not the God of Gentiles too? Yes, of Gentiles too, since there is only one God, who will justify the circumcised by faith and the uncircumcised through that same faith. (Romans 3:29–30)

> The sinful mind is hostile to God. It does not submit to God's law, nor can it do so. Those controlled by the sinful nature cannot please God. (Romans 8:7–8)

> So then, about eating food sacrificed to idols: We know that an idol is nothing at all in the world and that there is no God but one. For even if there are so-called gods, whether in heaven or on earth (as indeed there are many "gods" and many "lords"), yet for us there is but one God, the Father, from whom all things came and for whom we live; and there is but one Lord, Jesus Christ, through whom all things came and through whom we live. But not everyone knows this. Some people are still so accustomed to idols that when they eat such food they think of it as having been sacrificed to an idol, and since their conscience is weak, it is defiled. But food does not bring us near to God; we are no worse if we do not eat, and no better if we do. Be careful, however, that the exercise of your freedom does not become a stumbling block to the weak. For if anyone with a weak conscience sees you who have this knowledge eating in an idol's temple, won't he be emboldened to eat what has been sacrificed to idols? So this weak brother, for whom Christ died, is destroyed by your knowledge. (1 Corinthians 8:4–11)

> The spirits of prophets are subject to the control of prophets. For God is not a God of disorder but of peace. (1 Corinthians 14:32–33)

Do not be yoked together with unbelievers. For what do righteousness and wickedness have in common? Or what fellowship can light have with darkness? What harmony is there between Christ and Belial? What does a believer have in common with an unbeliever? What agreement is there between the temple of God and idols? For we are the temple of the living God. As God has said: "I will live with them and walk among them, and I will be their God, and they will be my people" (2 Corinthians 6:14–16).

Have you noticed the difference between the One True God and the gods of other religions? Their world and life is no different from ours. They are not objects or forces worthy of emulation. Folk religious practices provide a prominent place for the gods and other spiritual beings. There may be some well-meaning and good gods here and there portrayed in mythology, but these good gods also succumb to evil temptations.

As a relic of the non-Christian past, individuals born to Christian parents continue to be named after some gods and goddesses. *Diana*, for example, is a popular name among Westerners. I have deliberately retained my given Tamil Hindu name *Thirumalai*, which means "the Lord of the Sacred Hill." I adopt the meaning "the Lord of Zion" for my name; however, it still evokes the name of a Hindu god for the Hindus. They become curious when they learn that I am a Christian, and not a Hindu as my name suggests. I may therefore have an opening to talk to them about why I am a Christian. Even if I adopt a biblical proper name, still the problem would persist, because in my ethnic group your genealogy is part of your name. For example, my full name is Madasamy Subbiah Thirumalai: it means that Thirumalai is the son of Subbiah, and Subbiah is the son of Madasamy—Madasamy's son, Subbiah's son, Thirumalai. I can change my given name to a biblical one, but I cannot change the names of my father and grandfather, who were dead and gone before I accepted Jesus as my Lord and Savior.

The problems of the new Christian are many-sided. However, once our focus is on Jesus as Lord and Savior, these begin to lose their hold. The grace of Christ then abounds in our lives, and we begin to experience God in Spirit and in truth.

BIBLIOGRAPHY

Jamieson, R., A. Fausset, and D. Brown. "The Jamieson, Fausset, and Brown Commentary." In *The Bethany Parallel Commentary on the New Testament*. Minneapolis: Bethany House Publishers, 1983.

Monier-Williams, Monier. *Hinduism*. London: Society for Promoting Christian Knowledge, 1911.

Nave, Orville J. *The New Nave's Topical Bible*. Revised and compiled by Edward Viening. Grand Rapids, Mich.: Regency Reference Library, 1969.

Nicholls, Bruce J. "Hinduism." In Norman Anderson, ed. *The World's Religions*. Grand Rapids: Wm. B. Eerdmans Publishing Company, 1975, reprinted 1991.

Noss, John B. *Man's Religions*. New York: The Macmillan Company, 1969.

Schaff, Philip, ed. "Saint Augustine: Sermon on New Testament Lessons, Sermon 12." In *A Select Library of the Nicene and Post-Nicene Fathers of the Christian Church: Volume VI*. Grand Rapids: Eerdmans, reprinted 1991.

Srinivasan, T. N. *A Handbook of South Indian Images: An Introduction to the Study of Hindu Iconography*. Tirupati: Tirumalai-Tirupati Devasthanams, 1954.

Vine, W. E. *The Expanded Vine's Expository Dictionary of New Testament Words*. John R. Kohlenberger III, ed. Minneapolis: Bethany House, 1984.

Thank you for selecting a book from
BETHANY HOUSE PUBLISHERS

Bethany House Publishers is a ministry of Bethany Fellowship
International, an interdenominational, nonprofit organization
committed to spreading the Good News of Jesus Christ around
the world through evangelism, church planting, literature
distribution, and care for those in need. Missionary training is
offered through Bethany College of Missions.

Bethany Fellowship International is a member of the National
Association of Evangelicals and subscribes to its statement of
faith. If you would like further information, please contact:

Bethany Fellowship International
6820 Auto Club Road
Bloomington, MN 55438 USA

www.bethfel.org